BOWLS

of

PLENTY

ALSO BY CAROLYNN CARREÑO

Mozza at Home (with Nancy Silverton)

My Life on a Plate (with Kelis Rogers)

Taming the Feast (with Ben Ford)

Meat (with Pat LaFrieda)

The Mozza Cookbook (with Nancy Silverton)

One Pot

Sara Foster's Casual Cooking (with Sara Foster)

Twist of the Wrist (with Nancy Silverton)

Eat Me (with Kenny Shopsin)

Foods of the World: New York

Fresh Every Day (with Sara Foster)

100 Ways to Be Pasta (with Wanda and Giovanna Tornabene)

Once Upon a Tart (with Frank Mentesana and Jerome Audureau)

BOWLS
of
PLENTY

Recipes for Healthy and Delicious Whole-Grain Meals

Carolynn Carreño

Photographs by Beatriz da Costa
Foreword by Nancy Silverton

GRAND CENTRAL
Life & Style

New York Boston

Grand Central Life & Style
Hachette Book Group
1290 Avenue of the Americas, New York, NY 10104
grandcentrallifeandstyle.com
twitter.com/grandcentralpub

First Hardcover Edition: January 2017

Grand Central Life & Style is an imprint of Grand Central Publishing.
The Grand Central Life & Style name and logo are trademarks of
Hachette Book Group, Inc.

The publisher is not responsible for websites (or their content) that are not
owned by the publisher.

The Hachette Speakers Bureau provides a wide range of authors for
speaking events. To find out more, go to www.hachettespeakersbureau.com
or call (866) 376-6591.

Print book interior design by Amy Sly

Library of Congress Cataloging-in-Publication Data

Names: Carreño, Carolynn, author.
Title: Bowls of plenty : recipes for healthy and delicious whole-grain meals /
    Carolynn Carreno.
Description: First hardcover edition. | New York : Grand Central Life &
    Style, [2017] | Includes index.
Identifiers: LCCN 2016028808| ISBN 9781455536580 (hardcover) | ISBN
    9781455536573 (e-book)
Subjects: LCSH: Cooking (Cereals)
Classification: LCC TX808 .C365 2017 | DDC 641.6/31—dc23 LC record
    available at https://lccn.loc.gov/2016028808

ISBNs: 978-1-4555-3658-0 (hardcover), 978-1-4555-3657-3 (ebook)

Printed in the United States of America

Q-MA

10   9   8   7   6   5   4   3   2   1

This book is for the dedicated individuals out there who find the time to cook for themselves and their families and friends. Because despite what many people say, the food, and how and with what it's made, does matter.

CONTENTS

Foreword by Nancy Silverton..8

Introduction..13

Cooking From This Book..16

Shopping..19

Equipment, Tools, and Gadgets..25

Meet Your Grains..32

BREAKFAST BOWLS..49

SALAD BOWLS..89

MAIN BOWLS..116

DESSERT BOWLS..211

Acknowledgments..234

Index..235

FOREWORD

Nancy Silverton

My friend Carolynn Carreño has written three of my cookbooks and many others for chefs and food personalities around the country. She has always captured my voice and vision with clarity and elegance, and now, at long last, Carolynn has penned her very own cookbook, *Bowls of Plenty*, a wonderful collection that could not be published at a better time. The popularity of bowls is obvious. Drive down any Main Street, USA, visit any airport terminal or food court, and you'll see Bowl This and Bowl That. I know these bowls are supposed to be healthy, but since I cook and eat with only one thing in mind—*flavor*— I'm happy (but not surprised) to see that Carolynn's book is aimed at making sure these healthful, wholesome bowls will be as good tasting as they are good *for* you.

So "Bowls of Plenty" is the ideal concept for Carolynn's first cookbook, as she was an advocate of "bowling" long before eating healthy-delicious was all the rage. More than a dozen years ago, when we were first thrown together by our mutual agent to work on my book *Twist of the Wrist* (I was to develop the recipes and she was to write it) Carolynn was already singing the praises of healthy grain bowls, eating them at her favorite LA restaurant and snacking on crispy quinoa before I even knew what quinoa was.

Likewise, when Carolynn would tell me of her cooking adventures, it seemed like it always started with a bowl. A bowl of oatmeal, a bowl of rice, or a bowl of farro tossed with veggies and vinaigrette into a creative salad. Almost every time we collaborated on the phone, I would have to share Carolynn's attention—she would be stirring a pot of lentils or toasting almonds or interrupting my directions with a question such as how does my kitchen manager, Sal, make our staff lunch rice taste so good.

Although she is not a professional chef, the amount of information and technique Carolynn has gleaned by writing so many cookbooks—about a butcher, about baker, about a deli owner, about me—makes her uniquely qualified to write her own cookbook. This is evident in the clarity and detail of each recipe in *Bowls of Plenty*, and in the style and flavor combinations of the bowls themselves. Yes, she has the information of a professional, but Carolynn is ultimately a home cook: someone who cooks in a relatively small kitchen, without loads of time or a staff to help her. When we are working on my recipes, she frequently scolds me, reminding me that the cookbooks are for home cooks, not professionals, and that I have to adjust this or that so that someone doesn't kill herself trying to make a recipe. This has made my own books more user-friendly, and the same philosophy makes *Bowls of Plenty* the ultimate home cook's book.

Quite early on in our relationship, I came to realize Carolynn had a finely tuned palate and excellent taste. Many times when a dish didn't quite sing, Carolynn's adjustments to the recipe put it over the top. It was obvious I was not dealing with a just cookbook writer, but someone who had a great love for and knowledge of food. Over the years, I've also come to depend upon her as my right hand at dozens of parties at my homes in Los Angeles and in Umbria. I don't need to look over Carolynn's shoulder to see if she's doing something right. I know she is.

Carolynn can be very chatty, in a sweet way, like a kid so eager to tell you about something they learned at school. And this enthusiasm comes through in the small stories that proceed the recipes in *Bowls*. Check out "Grandmother Birdie's Oatmeal Cocktail" and you'll know exactly what I mean.

In days of yore, whole grains were thought of almost like vitamins, something that was good for you, but dull and without pleasure. Carolynn Carreño's *Bowls of Plenty: Recipes for Healthy and Delicious Whole-Grain Meals* destroys that notion. This book proves that in the right hands, whole-grain bowls can be absolutely delicious, full of texture, vibrant, fun, colorful, and imaginative. Oh yeah, and healthy. She did me proud.

BOWLS

of

PLENTY

INTRODUCTION

About a dozen years ago, I was dining at a Boston seafood restaurant owned by a renowned New England chef, when the server asked me, "How do you stay so skinny eating like this?" (Not that I am *so skinny*, but I do try to be *so healthy*.) The server was setting down several plastic baskets of fried food as she said it—it was that kind of seafood place. I was with my then editor at *Saveur* magazine, Colman Andrews, and he answered for me: "When she's not out, eating like this, she's home eating brown rice and broccoli."

It was true.

Colman said it with not a little bit of scorn, playfully trying to shame me. At the time, eating healthy was still frowned upon in the "gourmet" world. Eating *everything*, a hard-and-fast policy of not holding back, was the sign of a true epicurean warrior. Who would have thought that just a decade later we would be an entire nation of health-conscious foodies, and that bowls like those I was enjoying within the walls of my New York City apartment, wherein whole grains provides the virtuous base to tastier stuff piled on top, would be served everywhere, from national fast food chains to the most precious farm-to-table restaurants? This book is a collection of recipes for just such bowls, from the most humble and easy to prepare, to some that are a little more involved, and more decadent.

I like to think I come to the world of whole grains honestly. I grew up in the 1970s in Southern California, with a pseudo-hippie mother who drove a van with wall-to-wall shag carpet and made macramé plant hangers and stained glass windows in her spare time. Although she wasn't much for cooking, she billed herself as a "health nut," and wouldn't let us eat anything white. We would sooner have found a monkey in the house than a loaf of Wonder Bread. "It's just white flour and water," she would say. "No nutritional value!" Instead, she stocked the pantry with Oroweat Honey Wheat Berry bread, which was packed with chewy wheat berries and sunflower seeds (and is to this day my favorite base for avocado toast or to make French toast), and when my sister, Christy, and I would lobby for Froot Loops or Cap'n Crunch cereal, she would tell us, "You might as well eat a Hershey's bar for breakfast!" Well, okay… But except during s'mores season, those were off-limits, too. Instead, into the cart would go boxes of Quaker 100% Natural Granola, Kellogg's Raisin Bran, and jars of wheat germ, all of which, despite their hefty sugar content, made the cut because they *looked* natural. Venturing out into the world, when I was sixteen, I got my first job, filling the bulk bins at a natural food store. So although Uncle Ben's Long Grain and Wild Rice, complete with the cook's crutch of that era, "the flavor packet," was the only grain found in my house, and about as "whole grain" as that Hershey's bar, I was aware at an early age of the existence of foods like amaranth, barley, millet, and quinoa.

I started cooking whole grains myself about fifteen years ago, around the same time I started writing about food, which was long before words and phrases like "detox" and "eating clean" became part of our national culinary vocabulary. I did it for one simple reason: I wanted to feel good. Magazine assignments for *Saveur, Bon Appétit*, and *Gourmet* had me wandering the markets of Mexico City eating all manner of braised meats stuffed into corn tortillas and bound by melted cheese; or traveling through the Mississippi Delta subsisting on such local staples as lard-fried fruit hand pies, fried chicken livers, and lemon icebox pie. Back home in New York City, I was out several nights a week at the hottest new restaurants or food industry events, where I might sit down to a dinner that consisted of a series of rich, intricate morsels, each seeming harmless as I lifted a Chinese soup spoon to my lips, or popped a bite into my mouth, but lethal when there were twenty more such bites after that one. Even the freshest farmers' market vegetables were cooked in such a way as to absorb as much butterfat as the laws of physics would allow. After these nights, I would wake up with a food hangover. I felt tired. My mind was foggy. My stomach was bloated. And so it was that I retreated to a private life of brown rice and cruciferous vegetables, until the next night of foie gras this and truffled that. This was my style of yo-yo dieting.

Today, even though I can be found steaming brown rice or quinoa at least three times a week, I am a flavor-first cook. I come from a "gourmet" point of view, not a "health food" point of view. (In a nutshell, I eat blueberries because they taste good, not for the antioxidants they contain.) I've written cookbooks with and cooked in the kitchens of some of the most esteemed chefs in the country. And I have had the great privilege of eating in great restaurants, from barbecue joints in Alabama, Memphis, and Texas to the best restaurants in New York, Los Angeles, Italy, Mexico, and beyond. These experiences have informed my expectations. When I prepare a meal, I know how good that thing has the potential to taste and that's how I want *mine* to taste. I want my food to be so good that someone *might actually* write home about it. Which is all to say that I am not a "health food nut." I am a *food nut*. Granted, I am a food nut who wants to take care of my one and only body, and big bowls piled with grains, vegetables, beans, and small portions of animal protein are the way I have learned to do that. This book is a collection of those bowls, recipes that reflect the balance that I've learned to strike between wanting delicious food, and wanting to feel good—on a daily basis.

Although I never would have believed that my personal mechanism for coping with overly rich food would become a national phenomenon, now that it has, it seems almost obvious, or at least inevitable. The grain bowl is a reflection of our current attitude toward food. Yes, we're a nation of pork belly–obsessed food snobs, but we are also a nation that worships at the altar of healthy, and that believes there is virtue, salvation, eternal youth, and maybe even everlasting life in eating nutritious foods.

The grain bowl manages to straddle both that near religious passion we have for eating well and the great American desire to have it all— particularly if what we're having tastes terrific. In the grain bowl, and in the recipes in this book, we are literally able to have our cake and eat healthy, too.

COOKING FROM THIS BOOK

This book is broken up into four chapters. Breakfast Bowls includes sweet and savory grain bowls and whole-grain porridges; Salad Bowls are big bowls of grain salads loaded with vegetables and tossed with dressing; Main Bowls are meant to be main dishes; and Dessert Bowls are grains in sugary incarnations.

I thought about breaking up the Main Bowls into those with meat and those without, but decided against it, because bowls, being assembled of various components, are flexible. That's the beauty of bowls. With few—and I mean *few*—exceptions, you can make any bowl in this book vegetarian, and of course you can add animal protein to any vegetarian bowl—although the vegetarian bowls are so flavorful and substantial, you may not even want to. Many of the bowls are vegan, but they're also so full of flavor that even a die-hard meat eater won't notice the missing meat until they're halfway through the bowl.

Mix 'n' Match

In addition to the composed bowls that make up the Main Bowls chapter, I also encourage you to create your own custom bowls by mixing-and-matching from the various components—grains, proteins, vegetables, and condiments—in that chapter. But keep in mind that making a bowl is like going to a salad bar; if you put some thought into it and show some restraint, you'll end up with a better-tasting (and probably better-looking) bowl. To help you create the best combinations of ingredients, I've included four build-your-own spreads: Build Your Own Asian Bowl, Build Your Own Farmers' Market–Inspired Bowl, Build Your Own Middle Eastern Bowl, and Build Your Own Mexican Bowl. Choose any combination within each list and you're guaranteed a delicious result.

Entertaining with Grain Bowls

Having a dinner party? Construct a grain bowl buffet from among the build-your-own spreads. Choose one or two grains (make one gluten-free), one animal protein and one vegetarian option, a couple (or more) vegetables, and a few condiments. This way, you'll be catering to all your friends' and family's dietary needs and peculiarities, which is awfully nice of you, without actually having to hear about it, which, let's face it, is not that interesting.

The Recipes

When people ask me if I'm a chef, my usual response is, "I am a professional home cook." My recipes aren't chef recipes. Chef recipes often have ingredients lists so long it's as if they thought you lived in the grocery store, and they have so many steps that you'd need a battalion of prep cooks to get to the finish line. My recipes apply everything I've learned from chefs about how to make food as delicious as absolutely possible, but when I cook, I try to make things as easy as humanly possible.

What's more, the majority of people I spend time with on a regular basis are not in the food business. They're just regular people wanting to put healthy food on the table for themselves and their families on an ordinary weeknight, trying to figure out what foods to take to work to stay healthy and not break the bank, and hosting the occasional dinner party. I get texts nearly every day from friends and family members asking me what to make that night for dinner, what to substitute when they can't find an ingredient, what to serve for a party, or what kind of side dish to serve with whatever they're planning to cook. I wrote these recipes with those friends and family and their needs in mind.

SHOPPING

Mario Batali said it best when he said that the quality and deliciousness of your meal is already decided when you get home from shopping for that meal. What he means by that is, you can't make delicious food with less-than-delicious ingredients. So with Mario's words in mind, here are my thoughts on shopping:

Produce: I am a big proponent of buying local, seasonal produce, which means produce sold at farmers' markets. In-season produce is infinitely tastier than out-of-season produce because foods that are out of season are most often grown in faraway places, picked before they ripen, and shipped to their final destinations. Farmers' markets only sell seasonal fruit and vegetables because the farmers in the area grew those things, picked them or plucked them or pulled them from the ground at the time they are the most flavorful, packed them in crates, put them in a truck, drove them to the city, and set them out on a table to sell, like a kid with a lemonade stand. Old school, I know. Isn't it great?

Also, produce grown by small farmers is generally grown with flavor in mind. Farmers grow the tomatoes and green beans and lettuces and strawberries that have existed throughout time, and that taste like themselves. Industrially grown stuff, the stuff trucked and flown in from afar, is grown for money. These farmers manipulate crops so they can produce as much as possible, for as little money as possible, which they can sell for as much as possible. If these companies could make dead leaves look like a peach and sell it for $2 a pound, they would. But they can't. So instead they sell something that looks like a peach but tastes like dead leaves. Add to those reasons, you'll probably have a nice time shopping for the produce because farmers' markets are pleasant places to be. You never regret going. It's like taking an ocean swim or an evening walk. It sometimes takes some self-prodding, but you're always glad you did.

Even though I think that buying local and seasonal is the way to go, I'm not going to insist that there is no substitution—I've tried to lead that particular horse to water before and I know it doesn't work. Still, I do hope you'll start thinking the way the best cooks—home cooks and professionals—do: "Oh! It's asparagus season. Let me make something with asparagus!" I know that quality produce can sometimes be more expensive than shopping at most grocery stores, but you can also find good deals at farmers' markets, and here's why: Have you ever planted a tomato plant? You get about two thousand tomatoes, and they all ripen in the same week. You have to make friends with your entire zip code to get rid of them. Well, the same holds true for farmers. My friend Andy Arons, who owns a chain of gourmet grocery stores in Manhattan called Gourmet Garage, put it simply: "There's an inverse relationship between price and flavor." When blueberries are the most flavorful for a few weeks at the beginning of summer, he explains, they're at their lowest price. Why? Because blueberry farmers have tons of them, and they want to get rid of them. In the winter, blueberries are more expensive because they're being flown in from South America. And they don't taste like blueberries because in order to survive the journey from another continent, the berries have to be picked before they ripen, which means before the sugars and flavors in the fruit develop. No amount of time in a box or on a plane or sitting on your kitchen counter will ever change this fact. But for the sake of argument, let's say that the particular item you want *is* more expensive at the farmers' market than at the grocery store. Ask yourself this: Do you spend more money on what you put *on* your body, or *in* your body? And which do you think you *should* spend more money on? My point exactly.

Seafood: These days, when you go to the grocery store, you can be confronted with as many as four or five types of salmon alone. It's hard, I know. So how to know what to choose? My friend, the chef Jonathan Waxman, told me, "Never eat flying fish. If you're in California," he said, "eat fish from the Pacific. If you're in New York, eat fish from the Atlantic. It's so simple." If you have a seafood market near you, or a fishmonger at your farmers' market, shop there. Ask the people who work there about the fish they're selling or what might be the best substitute for a fish called for in a recipe. And if you really want to know more, visit the Monterey Bay Aquarium's very informative, user-friendly "seafood watch" page.

Pork: I have never seen the logic in saying that eating the meat of fish and chicken is good and eating the meat of steer, lamb, and pigs is, in that order bad to worse, so I consider the current pork- (and in particular, bacon-) embracing movement a step forward for the American culinary point of view. I especially believe that eating pork is a good thing when the pork you eat comes from heritage breeds of pigs, the most widely available of which is Kurobuta (aka Berkshire). In the 1970s, the commercial pork industry, as part of its "other white meat" campaign, which is one of the most successful ad campaigns of all time, began breeding the fat out of pork until eventually, and to this day, a conventionally raised pork loin had the same fat content as a skinless, boneless chicken breast. (Can we please pause to take a moment to imagine a pig with the same fat content as a small, feathery, walking bird?) Unfortunately, that pork also has the same amount of flavor as a chicken breast, which is somewhere near none. Heritage breeds, on the other hand, refer to original, heirloom breeds of pigs, meaning they were not genetically altered to be chicken-like; they grow up to be as they always were and as pigs are meant to be: fatty and flavorful. These pigs are also humanely raised on small farms; industrial farms don't go in for these less profitable breeds. When you cook heritage pork, you'll notice a difference in the color: it's darker and pinker and definitely *not* the other white meat. It's also considerably moister and more flavorful. You can find Kurobuta (and sometimes other heritage breeds) at quality butcher shops, high-end grocery stores with a good meat selection, and from online sources. It's more expensive than conventionally raised pork, but if you're going to eat animals, eat animals that had a happy, healthy life.

Lamb: I was not lamb's biggest fan until I wrote a book with celebrity butcher Pat LaFrieda and discovered that the reason I didn't like lamb was that I was eating the wrong lamb. I needed to eat American lamb, which he told me with no lack of confidence or national pride, is the best lamb in the world. Some is labeled "Sonoma lamb," some "Colorado lamb," but as long as the lamb is flying the stars and stripes, you're pretty much guaranteed it'll be tender with a mild, appealing flavor. The lamb that has the strong, gamey, goat-like flavor that I (and a lot of you) associate with lamb (and with our dislike of it), is imported from Australia and New Zealand. It's the lamb you find at standard grocery stores, discount grocery stores, and club stores. The inferior quality explains why it's half the price of American lamb, even though it traveled halfway around the planet. Since I am closer on the financial spectrum to a not-quite-starving artist than a free-spending mogul, I, too, have to worry about the price of groceries. My solution, where lamb is concerned, is to buy lamb less frequently and serve smaller portions. Half the lamb, half the price. Foodie math.

Beef: I don't love the taste of grass-fed beef; it's too bland and dry for me and I'd rather not eat beef than eat beef that I don't love. If you do love it, rock on. Proponents of grass-fed beef claim it's better for the planet and for you. But I love the great, bloody steak flavor of good ol' juicy, marbled American beef. How to justify eating this on a planet in distress? First, it's my understanding (again, per butcher Pat LaFrieda—I mean, what do I know about meat?) that even conventionally raised cattle are not fed grains their entire life. They eat grass for the first 85 percent of their life and are switched to grains in the last 15 percent, or four to five months. With that in mind, grass-fed beef is not oh so holier. So I eat the beef that tastes good to me. Also, I only, and I mean *exclusively*, buy beef from a good source. I'm lucky to have a wonderful butcher near where I live; not a modern butcher, hatched from the young butchering craze, but an old-school take-a-number shop serviced by a bunch of friendly guys who know my name and everything, it seems, there is to know about meat. They sell the highest quality prime meat, and they don't sell any meat containing hormones or antibiotics. I also buy my bacon there, and, if you must know, ground chicken, bones and all, for my adorable, GMO- and antibiotic-free miniature Labradoodle, Rufus.

Chicken: Have you ever been to a conventional chicken farm? Or seen one in a documentary? Google it now. You'll never look at chicken the same way again. You'll see: the chickens are crowded into pens. They live a life where they never, *never*, roam free. At many farms, they aren't even allowed sunlight or fresh air. They are bred to have such large breasts that mostly they just sit, or rather, squat, around. And they're squatting in a bed of feces, which is often not cleaned for years, which explains why chicken farms are the worst smelling places on planet earth. Why, it's enough to make you look for free-range chicken, isn't it? Look for chicken that is GMO-free, and free of antibiotics. Mary's Chicken is a good, safe bet, and widely available. Chicken at farmers' markets is expensive; if you're willing to fork over the money, you'll be rewarded with flavor and good karma.

Eggs: There are certain things that really are better when bought at a farmers' market, and eggs are one of them. Farm-fresh eggs have so much flavor that once you start eating them, you won't know what that other egg-shaped thing you've been eating all your life was. And the color! The yolks are a bright, goldenrod yellow. For perfectly cooked eggs, see Eggs Every Which Way (page 58). And as any grain bowl-er knows, a fried egg on a bowl of grains, especially grains that are spiced up and dressed with other ingredients, is dinner, and a perfectly boiled egg can turn any combination into a beauty bowl. Don't you think the egg should be *great*?

EQUIPMENT, TOOLS, AND GADGETS

The late, great food writer Laurie Colwin once wrote something to the effect of, "I feel sorry for anybody who picks up a cookbook only to find a list of equipment you need to buy in order to cook from it." This isn't that. What this is, instead, is a randomly organized list of those tools and gadgets and vessels that I constantly reach for. Because here's the thing. I often find myself cooking at other people's houses, and more often than not, they have such a haphazard collection of tools and cooking equipment, and I think, *No wonder you don't like to cook.* Cooking without the right tools can be so uncomfortable and frustrating. The items on this list, many of which are very inexpensive, make cooking easier and more fun for me, and I'm including them here in case it will make cooking more fun for you, too.

1. **Microplane:** Throw away your garlic presses, everyone. They don't work that well. Cleaning the minuscule garlic bits out of the tiny holes is virtually impossible. And besides, the Microplane, which is a kitchen tool that originated as a tool-tool (a rasp) makes such easy work of grating garlic. It works for grating ginger, too. And for grating cheese over a dish. But the garlic thing—it's going to change your life. In these recipes, I call for number of cloves rather than measurements because I like to grate the garlic directly into whatever vessel I'm adding it to; besides, who wants to spend their time stuffing grated garlic into a teeny spoon?

2. **Scissors:** These are invaluable in the kitchen, for opening packages, cutting off carrot tops, and most essentially, snipping herbs. I have a Wustoff pair, but my favorite scissors are a red handled pair I paid $4 for at the Asian grocer.

3. **Mandoline:** For thinly slicing and shaving vegetables. You need one if you're going to make shaved raw vegetable salads, such

as Shaved Brussels Sprouts with Spelt, Walnuts, and Pecorino (page 98). They also come in handy for cutting vegetables into delicate matchsticks and/or dicing very small. The good news is, inexpensive plastic mandolines are widely available.

4. **Mini food processor:** For pureeing chipotle chiles, grinding nuts, making pesto, and grating chunks of hard cheese, such as Parmesan or Pecorino. They're inexpensive, easy to use, and lightweight. I have two.

5. **Vitamix or another stellar blender:** For whirring up sauces, hummus, pesto, and other purees. I inherited one used, so it's not very pretty. Nevertheless, it opened up my cooking world.

6. **Cast-iron griddle or grill pan:** I'm madly in love with my long, rectangular Lodge cast-iron griddle/grill. It fits over two burners, and it is a griddle on one side and a grill pan with grill grates on the other. The grill side allows me to grill even when I don't feel like going outside and lighting a fire. I use the griddle side for making pancakes, warming tortillas, and searing meats. The griddle, being flat, provides more surface area, which means more brown deliciousness. It cost me $60 at Sur La Table and it has already paid for itself as far as I'm concerned.

7. **Baking sheets:** I suggest you have a lot of these, and preferably *not* nonstick. I recommend sheet pans, which are thick, with sides about ¾ inch tall. Thin-gauge cookie sheets buckle in the oven. Thick ones, and those that develop patina over time, will give you more color on your vegetables. I buy them in packs of two at Sur La Table. I most often use the half sheet pan size (18 by 13 inches) for tasks like roasting vegetables, but I also have quarter sheet pans (9 by 13 inches) for small jobs like toasting nuts. The nice thing about these is that they stack, so you can keep a lot of them in a small space, which is essential since my kitchen is smaller than your average walk-in closet.

8. **Bowls:** Having plenty of mixing and prep bowls on hand makes life so much easier. I like sets of small bowls for holding prepped quantities of little things like herbs and garlic, and I have an extensive set of stainless-steel bowls for tossing grains and salads. I buy them at kitchen supply stores. They're not expensive, light, and don't break. And they nest, so they only take as much space as your largest bowl.

9. **Fish spatula:** A so-called fish spatula is made of metal and is thin and flexible, so you can really get under something and turn it without leaving the nice browned part behind in the pan. For me, it's not just for fish anymore. It's the only spatula (other than a rubber spatula) I will ever need.

10. **Dutch oven:** Heavy, large pots for braising and making beans and soup. I love my Staub pots for their sheer beauty but I also have a giant, vintage Le Creuset that I inherited from my dad and two less expensive Mario Batali by Dansk pots from Bed Bath & Beyond. Honestly, they all work the same, and I use them all, all the time.

11. **Rubber spatulas:** Essential in dessert making, for scraping the good stuff off the sides of the bowls, and also for cleaning out blenders, making scrambled eggs and stir-fries, stirring sauces and porridges (many rubber spatulas are heatproof), and folding salad ingredients together without any smashing and breaking. I have several, and when I'm cooking a big meal, I use every one.

12. **Food-handling gloves:** Using your hands to toss salads and perform other jobs in the kitchen is, in my opinion, an essential and enjoyable part of cooking. Gloves are for those who want to get down and dirty in the kitchen but without the dirty.

13. **Tongs:** For turning things, like vegetables, in a skillet or on a baking sheet. When you want to really achieve that perfect caramelization that makes food look and taste delicious,

shaking or stirring can only do so much. You have to take the 45 seconds it requires to turn every last mushroom, each Brussels sprout, or each shrimp. Tongs are the only way to get the job done.

14. **Pots and pans:** I'm an All-Clad girl. I have a collection of the least expensive line in New York, and one set of the classic, mid-priced line in California; and I can tell the difference by the weight of the pans, but barely. One of the things I like about doing the matchy-matchy thing with my pots and pans, besides the fact that it satisfies my slight OCD leanings, is that the lids to same-width pots are interchangeable. Here are the pieces that I couldn't, or wouldn't want to, live without: A straight-sided skillet with a lid is my go-to for no-fail, fluffy, and perfectly cooked grains. I use a smallish (2-quart) saucepan, which I call my oatmeal pan, almost daily for making porridge. I use my 3-quart All-Clad saucier, which looks like a stainless-steel bowl with two handles and a lid, for making porridge when I want more room, for cooking soup, larger batches of saucy things, and sautéing just about anything. I invested in a proper All-Clad stockpot only recently; it makes clean and easy work of cooking chicken or vegetable stock because it means not having to turn over a giant pot to strain out bones or vegetables; instead, those things go in an insert, like pasta in a pasta cooker, and you lift them out in one quick, easy motion. I once stood firmly and stubbornly in the anti-nonstick pan camp. Then, in the last couple of years, I bought one for cooking eggs and fish. It's been life altering. I now cook many more eggs and much more fish, both in much less oil than I would have had to in another pan.

15. **Wire whisk:** Essential for whipping, stirring, mashing, and, of course, whisking.

16. **Knives:** I'm sorry to disappoint you by telling you this, but you don't need a knife block. And you don't need a set. I know that the knife block knife set is part and parcel of the American dream, but they take up valuable counter space, and you won't use half of them. Serious professional cooks buy one knife that they love. Then they buy another knife that they love. And then another… The knives don't even match, if you can imagine! You only really need two knives: a big knife, called a chef's knife, and a small paring knife. I love my Shun chef's knife, which was a gift from Sara Foster, a wonderful cook with whom I have written two cookbooks. And my Global vegetable cleaver, which was a gift from me to myself. And I rely heavily on my inexpensive, plastic-handled Victorinox paring knife, which I got from Nina Maconnell's wonderful weekend pop-up shop at Chino Ranch. Buy what feels good in your hand. Most important: Keep your knives sharp. That long round thing that makes you feel like a samurai using it? That's called a honing steel. Its job is to realign the edge of the blade, which does make it a little sharper. But real knife sharpening requires special skills. Unless you have them, take your knife to a knife sharpener. (There is no shame in not sharpening your own knives. Knife sharpeners make regular rounds to restaurant kitchens, sharpening the knives of chefs.)

17. **Plastic U-shaped vegetable peelers:** These are so superior to the straight ones that I grew up using, and they're only about five bucks apiece. My favorites are Kuhn Rikon Swiss Peelers, which come in a revolving variety of bright colors. I buy them in packs of three, and I often give them as gifts.

18. **Recycled jam jars, deli containers, and plastic zip-top bags:** To store all that delicious homemade food you'll be cooking from this book. Cooking up big batches of grains, beans, and condiments to mix and match for last-minute meal preparation is the secret to home-cooking success.

19. **Strainer:** I have one that fits across my sink, which, in a small kitchen, is life altering. I use it for rinsing vegetables, beans, and grains. Then I have a set of handheld fine-mesh strainers. In a grain bowl world, you will need the large one for rinsing and draining grains. Keep it handy.

20. **Mexican elbow:** That's a new term for me, not used (that I know of) in Mexico, where actual Mexican elbows are everywhere. I'm referring to that hinged gadget in which you put a half a lime for squeezing the juice (I call it a lime squeezer). I have one for lemons, too. Very handy, but positively indispensable when juicing large amounts of lemons or limes, such as for making vinaigrettes or *micheladas*, beer and lime juice cocktails, when all's said and done.

MEET YOUR GRAINS

What Is a Whole Grain?

A whole grain is a grain consisting of three parts: the bran (the fiber-rich outermost layer), the germ (the small core that is rich in antioxidants, vitamins, and healthy fats), and the endosperm. Together, the bran and germ contain about a quarter of a grain's protein. Refined grains are stripped of those outer layers so that just the endosperm remains. Thus, the grain goes from being a *healthy carb*, to just a carb, still offering protein (and calories), but little else.

Whole grains have been a staple in the human diet for thousands of years; only in the last hundred years have refined, processed grains (white rice, pearl barley, all-purpose flour) become the norm. The 1873 invention of the roller mill allowed for the efficient separation of the bran and germ from the endosperm. This was initially done to improve the grain's shelf life. Exporters liked the longer shelf life. Consumers liked the taste. And refined grains and flours became the thing.

Health Benefits of Whole Grains

There are countless health benefits of eating whole grains as opposed to refined grains—and no downside. Whole grains are digested more slowly than refined grains, keeping insulin and blood sugar levels down. Eating whole grains also contributes to a lower mortality rate, lower risk of type 2 diabetes, reduced risk of heart disease, lower cholesterol levels, reduced blood pressure, reduced risk of stroke, and reduced risk of cancer, especially cancers of the digestive system.

So now that you see that whole grains are your friend, following is a list of grains (and a few seeds, such as quinoa, that live life as grains), including for each grain a definition and description, information on how to cook it, and best uses for that grain. What I don't do is tell you that this grain is higher in protein and that one has more antioxidants, because I don't believe in eating foods just for the specific nutrients they contain. Instead, I believe you should eat a diet rich in real food—foods that come from the ground and are still in the state in which they were grown—including whole grains, vegetables, and fruits, with animal proteins in side dish portions. I don't think eating healthy needs or should be any more complicated.

AMARANTH

Amaranth is a gluten-free seed that is cooked and treated as a grain; it tastes a bit like corn that has been boiled for too long. Cooked, amaranth turns gelatinous and gummy (*no bueno*), so I use it in places where that texture can be hidden, such as in a porridge. If you want the corny flavor of amaranth without the texture, substitute ¼ cup amaranth in place of the quinoa in any quinoa recipe. You can also pop amaranth in a skillet, which gives it a mild, toasty flavor. Amaranth is commonly prepared this way in its native land, Mexico, where it's subsequently used to make candy—think sesame brittle, only an amaranth version—and it's often added to granola and other crunchy snacks. I don't rinse amaranth before cooking it. It's too small and would fall through the holes of any strainer I own. While I'm here, I should tell you that amaranth is also a leafy green vegetable; the seeds come from the flowers of the plant. You may find it at Indian or Middle Eastern markets or farmers' markets. If you do, buy it and cook it up with garlic and olive oil, as if it were spinach.

BARLEY

Hulled barley is a whole grain, and contains gluten. It has an earthy flavor and chewy texture. The word "hulled" can be misleading; this means the tough outer hull has been removed, but the hull is removed from all grains before eating them, unless you're a bird—think about the hull of a sunflower seed. Pearl barley is barley that has been polished, or stripped of the bran. It cooks in half the time, but what's the purpose of eating barley if it's not nutritious?

Refrigerate cooked barley and use it to make salads such as Broccolini and Sprout Salad with Poppy Seed Dressing (page 111); plop a spoonful on top of a cup of yogurt with a spoonful of jam and granola; or make a quick savory breakfast yogurt with fresh herbs (such as parsley, oregano, mint, marjoram, basil, and/or chives) and harissa or Sriracha. It will last for a week. *Makes about 3 cups*

1 cup hulled or pearl barley, rinsed

1½ teaspoons kosher salt

Bring 6 cups water to a boil in a medium saucepan over high heat. Add the barley and salt and return the water to a boil. Reduce the heat to maintain a simmer and cook, uncovered, until the barley is tender, about 50 minutes for hulled barley, 25 minutes for pearl barley. Drain the barley and serve, or transfer to a wide bowl or baking sheet to cool to room temperature if you're cooking it to use in a salad.

BLACK RICE

The most common type of black rice is a medium-grain rice often referred to by the brand name Forbidden Rice. It turns dark purple when cooked and has a sweet, nutty unique flavor that makes Coconut Black and Wild Rice Pudding (page 212) special. You can also use black rice to make Ginger Scallion Rice (page 135), or in place of brown rice to serve with any Asian-leaning dish.

Black rice will keep for a week in the refrigerator. Heat leftovers with coconut milk to make a quick last-minute hot cereal; spoon it atop coconut yogurt and top with tropical fruit; or stir-fry it with ginger, garlic, soy sauce, and green veggies. All rice is gluten free. *Makes about 3½ cups*

1 cup black rice, rinsed

1 teaspoon kosher salt

Combine the rice, salt, and 3 cups water in a large straight-sided sauté pan and bring the water to a boil over high heat. Reduce the heat to low, cover, and simmer the rice for 20 to 30 minutes, until the liquid has been absorbed and the rice is tender. Turn off the heat and let the rice rest, covered, for 10 minutes. Uncover and fluff gently with a fork. Serve, or transfer the rice to a wide bowl or baking sheet to cool to room temperature if you're cooking it to use in a salad.

BROWN RICE (LONG-GRAIN)

Long-grain rice (which includes basmati, an aromatic Indian rice, and jasmine, an aromatic Thai rice) is thin and when cooked correctly, the grains don't stick together. Being able to cook up a good pot of long-grain brown rice is essential to your grain bowl future, because brown rice is the heart and soul of the grain bowl world. At least, it is to mine. Brown rice became my gateway food to good health and what is known today as "clean" eating. Every time I eat a bowl of freshly steamed rice, whether it's topped with curry, stir-fry, black beans, or poached salmon, I am reminded how much I enjoy eating it, and how great I feel *after* eating it. In a sense, it is the reason for this book. Thanks, brown rice.

The best way I've found to cook brown rice, which I now apply to any grains that are steamed (cooked with the lid on), is in a skillet with straight sides. This gives you more surface area than the more commonly used saucepan. More surface area means the rice turns out fluffier. It also helps the rice cook more evenly and faster. I rinse all grains before cooking them, but it's particularly important to rinse brown rice. In recent years, the Food and Drug Administration has reported that brown rice contains traces of arsenic. (From the Department of: If It's Not One Thing, It's Another.) Rinsing the rice can help reduce the levels of arsenic by as much as 30 percent.

Cooked brown rice will keep, refrigerated, for up to a week. With a little creativity and the recipes that lie ahead, having that cooked rice at your fingertips can make the difference between nothing to eat and dinner on the table. Use the cooked grains to make Quick and Easy Breakfast Fried Quinoa (page 53) or Red Rice Pad Thai (page 182; it's okay if the rice isn't red). Cooked rice is also used as a g-free binder for Pomegranate-Glazed Lamb Meatballs (page 183). So make more than you think you'll need. All rice is gluten free. *Makes about 3½ cups*

1 cup long-grain brown rice, rinsed

1 teaspoon kosher salt

Combine the rice, salt, and 2 cups water in a large straight-sided sauté pan and bring the water to a boil over high heat. Reduce the heat to low, cover, and simmer the rice for 20 to 30 minutes, until all the liquid has been absorbed and the rice is tender. Turn off the heat and let the rice rest, covered, for 10 minutes. Uncover and fluff gently with a fork. Serve, or transfer the rice to a wide bowl or baking sheet to cool to room temperature if you're cooking it to use in a salad.

BROWN RICE (SHORT-GRAIN)

Short-grain brown rice is shorter than long-grain rice, and almost round in shape. When cooked, the grains get soft and clump together. I like to use it when making things where soft and clumpy are positive characteristics, like for making Slow-Cooked Brown Rice and Quinoa Porridge (page 68) and Sorghum Risotto Primavera with Bacon and Burrata (page 205). All rice is gluten free. *Makes about 3 cups*

1 cup brown rice

1 teaspoon kosher salt

Combine the rice, salt, and 1¾ cups water in a large straight-sided sauté pan and bring the water to a boil over high heat. Reduce the heat to low, cover, and simmer the rice for about 45 minutes, until the liquid has been absorbed. Turn off the heat and let the rice rest, covered, for 10 minutes. Use a rubber spatula or wooden spoon to give the rice a tumble before serving. Serve the rice or transfer to a wide bowl or baking sheet to cool to room temperature if you're cooking it to use in a salad.

BUCKWHEAT

In the gluten-phobic world in which we live, buckwheat needs to think about rebranding itself, because, despite its name, it is *not* wheat, and it *is* gluten-free. Buckwheat groats (which are technically seeds), have an unusual shape—sort of like pyramids, or minuscule teeth and an earthy flavor and a crunchy, nugget-like texture. I don't love buckwheat cooked. It reminds me of something you'd eat in a cold Russian winter when you didn't have a lot of options. I love it toasted, however. And when it's toasted with sweetener as it is in Rosemary Buckwheat Crunch (page 70), I am obsessed. In the hot cereal aisle, you'll also see buckwheat that has been milled to the size of Cream of Wheat, which makes a hearty, earthy-tasting breakfast porridge. Or use it as a base for a breakfast rice bowl or as a more nutritious, higher-in-fiber alternative to the cornmeal in Millet Polenta (page 129).

BULGUR WHEAT

Bulgur, traditional to Middle Eastern cooking, is hard wheat (so it contains gluten) that has been boiled, dried, and cracked. Because it is precooked, it takes only 10 minutes to prepare. The cracked quality gives it an interesting, almost porous texture that really absorbs the flavors around it. Most people know bulgur for its role in tabbouleh, but it's a very versatile grain and can be used to make porridge (cook it with almond milk and cinnamon and serve with toasted almonds); instead of spelt to make the Shaved Brussels Sprouts with Spelt, Walnuts, and Pecorino (page 98); or in place of the farro in Summer Corn Farrotto with Brown Butter and Burst Sweet Tomatoes (page 144); or as a base for any grain bowl, particularly those with a Mediterranean vibe. As you can see, I'm a fan of bulgur. *Makes about 3 cups*

1 cup bulgur, rinsed

2 teaspoons kosher salt

Bring 3 cups water to a boil in a medium saucepan over high heat. Add the bulgur and salt. Reduce the heat to medium-high and gently boil the bulgur, uncovered, until it is tender but not mushy, 12 to 15 minutes. Drain the bulgur and serve, or transfer to a wide bowl or baking sheet to cool to room temperature if you're cooking it to use in a salad.

FARRO

Farro is an Italian word for specific varieties of wheat grains also known as einkorn (*farro piccolo*), emmer (*farro medio*), and spelt (*farro grande*). All are chewy and hearty, similar to barley. *Farro medio*, an ancient, unhybridized grain also called "true farro," is what I am referring to when I call for farro in these recipes. All farro varieties can be used interchangeably, and hulled barley and wheat berries, which have the same chewy characteristics as farro, can be used in their place. The majority of farro you will find, and what I call for in these recipes, is semi-pearled, which means the bran has been removed. If you manage to find and buy whole farro, which is available only at very few specialty stores and online sources, note that it will take about twice the time to cook. Some people swear by toasting farro before boiling it. I can go either way, but honestly, I don't think I can tell the difference in the flavor. Farro is not gluten-free although many believe that unadulterated grains such as farro are easier to digest for the gluten challenged.

Farro is a handy grain to have around to toss into salads, such as the Umbrian Farro and Bean Salad with Celery Leaf Pesto and Mozzarella (page 103), or in place of the rice in Italian Antipasto Rice Salad (page 95), to make a dessert of Dark Chocolate Farro Goop with Toasted Walnuts Steamed Cream (page 228), to add to a finished soup or stew, or to make a quick breakfast, spooned over yogurt with honey and fresh or dried figs. *Makes about 3 cups*

1 cup farro, rinsed

2 teaspoons kosher salt

If you are toasting the farro, adjust the oven racks so one is in the middle position and preheat the oven to 350°F.

Line a baking sheet with parchment paper, if you have it, and spread the farro out over the baking sheet. Toast the farro in the oven for 10 minutes, shaking the pan once or twice during that time so it toasts evenly.

Bring 6 cups water to a boil in a medium saucepan over high heat. Add the salt and farro, reduce to maintain a gentle boil, and cook, uncovered, until the farro is tender but still chewy, 25 to 30 minutes. Drain the farro and serve, or transfer to a wide bowl or baking sheet to cool to room temperature if you're cooking it to use in a salad.

FREEKEH

Freekeh is an Arab grain product made from durum wheat grains. The grains are harvested while they are still green, then sun-dried, roasted, and polished. In the Middle East, freekeh is sold whole or cracked, but in the United States, you'll only find it cracked. It looks like green bulgur and has an intense smoky flavor from the roasting. Because it derives from wheat, freekeh does contain gluten, but some speculate that the treatment of the grains denatures the gluten, making it more easily tolerated by those sensitive to gluten. I love the green color and roasted flavor of freekeh in the Pomegranate Tabbouleh (page 168); it would also be delicious in place of millet in the Rainbow Carrot Salad with Millet, Feta, and Lemon Yogurt Dressing (page 93). I wouldn't recommend it for a sweet porridge, but beyond that, let your freekeh imagination run wild. *Makes about 3 cups*

1 cup freekeh, rinsed

2 teaspoons kosher salt

Bring 3 cups water to a boil in a medium saucepan over high heat. Add the freekeh and salt, reduce the heat to medium-high, and gently boil the freekeh, uncovered, until it is tender, 12 to 15 minutes. Drain the freekeh and serve, or transfer to a wide bowl or baking sheet to cool to room temperature if you're cooking it to use in a salad.

KANIWA

You think quinoa's small? Kaniwa, a high-protein, gluten-free seed native to the Andes mountains in Bolivia and Peru, is about half quinoa's size. Cooked, kaniwa is crunchy, with the pop-in-your-mouth texture like the tiny fish eggs that coat a cut sushi roll. Kaniwa is even more nutrient dense than quinoa and comes in only one color: reddish brown. Use it in place of any of the other grains in the Four Grain "Nutella" Porridge (page 64). Or cook it on its own and combine it with other gluten-free grains, such as the quinoa in Red Beet and Quinoa Salad (page 96) or the Sambal Tofu Quinoa Bowl (page 119). Kaniwa is too small to rinse in any strainer I own; plus, unlike its cousin, quinoa, kaniwa does not have saponins on the exterior, which is what makes rinsing quinoa so important. *Makes about 1½ cups*

½ cup kaniwa
½ teaspoon kosher salt

Combine the kaniwa, salt, and 1½ cups water in a small saucepan and bring the water to a boil over high heat. Reduce the heat to low, cover the pan, and gently simmer the kaniwa for 20 minutes, until the liquid has been absorbed. Turn off the heat and let the kaniwa rest, covered, for 10 minutes. Uncover and fluff gently with a fork. Serve, or transfer the kaniwa to a wide bowl or baking sheet to cool to room temperature if you're cooking it to use in a salad.

KHORASAN WHEAT

Commonly sold under the trademarked name Kamut, Khorasan wheat is an ancient variety about twice the length of standard American wheat. The name comes from the region in Iran where the grains supposedly originate; Khorasan wheat has also been discovered in ancient Egyptian tombs. All to say that while it may be new to you, it is not new. Khorasan wheat takes over an hour to cook. The benefits? It has a rich flavor and wonderful, super chewy texture, is 30 percent higher in protein than modern American wheat, and is an unadulterated crop, which means it's free of genetic modification and other abuse, though it does contain gluten. *Makes about 2 cups*

1 cup Khorasan wheat (Kamut), rinsed
2 teaspoons kosher salt

Bring 6 cups water to a boil in a medium saucepan over high heat. Add the Khorasan wheat and salt. Reduce the heat to medium-high and gently boil the grains, uncovered, until they are tender but still chewy, 60 to 70 minutes. Drain and serve, or transfer the grains to a wide bowl or baking sheet to cool to room temperature if you're cooking them to use in a salad.

MILLET

Millet is a gluten-free grain (technically a seed) that most of us have known, even if not by name, for its role as the main ingredient in birdseed. Millet is a good source of protein, fiber, and other nutrients, and has been a staple in India and Africa for thousands of years; it has gained popularity here in the last decade, as more and more Americans strayed away from gluten. Cooked, millet can get gooey and gummy, which doesn't matter when it is cooked into a porridge, such as Four Grain "Nutella" Porridge (page 64) or Coconut Millet Porridge (page 80). But I have also perfected a method for cooking millet that results in grains that are fluffy and not sticky at all, like the whole-grain version of couscous. And you don't have to boil millet to eat it; you can also eat millet raw or toasted; I make Toasted Millet Frozen Custard (page 230) and I've also been known to throw it into chocolate chip cookie dough and Sweet and Salty Granola (page 75). *Makes about 4 cups*

1 cup hulled millet, rinsed

1 teaspoon kosher salt

Adjust the oven racks so one is in the middle position and preheat the oven to 350°F.

Bring 1¾ cups water to a boil in a large ovenproof sauté pan (FYI: most sauté pans are ovenproof, even those with rubber handles) over high heat. Add the millet and salt, and return the liquid to a boil. Turn off the heat and put the lid on the pan. Put the pan in the oven for 25 to 30 minutes, until the millet has absorbed all the liquid. Remove the millet from the oven and let it sit, covered, for 5 to 10 minutes; uncover and fluff gently with a fork. Serve or transfer to a wide bowl or baking sheet to cool to room temperature if you're cooking the millet to use in a salad.

OATS

Oats are a gluten-free grain native to Europe; their distinct, toasty flavor comes from the fact that the grains are roasted after being harvested. Oats come in a variety of forms: whole grains, which are called whole oat groats, steel-cut (also called Irish oats or Scottish oats), rolled oats, and quick-cook oats. You don't see whole oat groats often; they can be used in place of any chewy grain such as the farro in Spiced Apple Breakfast Farro (page 72), Summer Corn Farrotto Sweet (page 144), or Dark Chocolate Farro Goop (page 228). Steel-cut oats, whole oats that have been chopped into two or three pieces, are used to make porridge. Rolled oats have been steamed and then passed through a

roller to flatten them. Quick-cooked oats (aka "instant oats") are rolled oats that have been chopped up for quicker cooking. All have the same nutritional value, though instant oats have a higher glycemic index because the body processes them more quickly. Oats have more fiber than any other grain and are considered among the healthiest grains; they have a unique status in that companies may claim on the packaging that eating oats can help reduce the risk of heart disease.

QUINOA

Native to Peru, quinoa is the gluten-free seed of a plant, related to beets and Swiss chard (go figure!). Quinoa has had a meteoric rise in popularity over the last decade because it has a delicious, mild flavor, is packed with nutrients, and is a great source of protein. When cooked correctly, it has a light, fluffy, and totally appealing texture. Quinoa is coated with saponins, phytochemicals that can impart a bitter taste to cooked quinoa, so while some manufacturers remove this outer layer, it's still wise to rinse quinoa before cooking it. Quinoa grains can be white, red, or black. They taste the same, so which color you pick is a matter of style.

I almost always have cooked quinoa in the refrigerator. I mix it with a little sugar and cinnamon and serve it as a quick, healthy breakfast cereal with goji berries and raw cashews, or I use it to make Quick and Easy Breakfast Fried Quinoa (page 53). *Makes about 3½ cups*

1 cup quinoa, rinsed

1 teaspoon kosher salt

Combine the quinoa, salt, and 2 cups water in a large sauté pan and bring the water to a boil over high heat. Reduce the heat to low, cover, and gently simmer the quinoa until the water has been absorbed, about 20 minutes. Turn off the heat and let the quinoa rest, covered, for 10 minutes. Uncover and fluff gently with a fork. Serve, or transfer the quinoa to a wide bowl or baking sheet to cool to room temperature if you're cooking it to use in a salad.

RED RICE

Red rice is a long-grain rice from Southeast Asia. It is similar in texture and taste to brown rice but the exterior, or bran, of the rice is red, which is what gives the rice its unique color. There are many types of red rice, including heirloom Bhutanese rice, Himalayan red rice, and Thai red rice, sometimes sold as "red cargo rice," referring to the fact that it was shipped in cargo containers and packaged at its point of destination. The cooking time given here is for red cargo rice. Refer to the cooking times on the package if you are using a different variety of red rice. All rice is gluten-free. *Makes about 3½ cups*

1 cup red rice, rinsed

1 teaspoon kosher salt

Combine the rice, salt, and 1¾ cups water in a large sauté pan and bring the water to a boil over high heat. Reduce the heat to low, and cover. Simmer the rice until the water has been absorbed, about 30 minutes. Turn off the heat and let the rice sit, covered, for 10 minutes. Uncover and fluff gently with a fork. Serve, or transfer the rice to a wide bowl or baking sheet to cool to room temperature if you're cooking it to use in a salad.

RYE

Rye, a grain common to Russia and eastern European countries, is related to barley and wheat and, like those grains, contains gluten. The rye grain comes in many forms: Rye berries, whole rye grains, look like long, slender wheat berries. They can be used in place of wheat berries or other chewy grains, including farro, spelt, and Khorasan wheat. Cracked rye is the equivalent of cracked wheat, or bulgur; cook cracked rye as if it were bulgur. Rye flakes look like large rolled oats, but with a darker, grayish hue and an earthier flavor. Use them in any recipe that calls for rolled oats, such as to make a quick breakfast cereal, or in place of or in combination with rolled oats in Sweet and Salty Granola (page 75) or Whole-Grain Crisp Topping (page 216). *Makes about 2 cups*

1 cup rye berries, rinsed

2 teaspoons kosher salt

Bring 6 cups water to a boil in a medium saucepan over high heat. Add the rye berries and salt. Reduce the heat to medium-high and gently boil the rye berries, uncovered, until they are tender but still chewy, 60 to 70 minutes. Drain the rye berries and serve, or transfer to a wide bowl or baking sheet to cool to room temperature if you're cooking them to use in a salad.

SORGHUM

Sorghum, a round, gluten-free grain, is a staple grain in Africa and India. It has a mild flavor, so it reminds me of little round pasta such as Israeli couscous, but with loads of nutritional value. Sorghum takes a long time to cook, and seems to be impossible to overcook, so it's the perfect grain to toss into soup. Soaking the grains overnight helps to reduce their cooking time. It has a chewy texture, so it's the ideal g-free substitute for other chewy grains such farro, spelt, and wheat berries *Makes about 2 cups*

1 cup sorghum, preferably soaked overnight and drained

1 tablespoon kosher salt

Bring 2 quarts water to a boil over high heat. Add the sorghum and salt, reduce the heat to medium-high, and gently boil the sorghum, uncovered, until tender, about 50 minutes. (If you did not soak the sorghum, keep cooking until they are tender, adding more water as necessary; it might take 70 minutes or more.) Drain and serve, or transfer the sorghum to a wide bowl or baking sheet to cool to room temperature if you are cooking it to use in a salad.

SPELT

Spelt, known in Italy as *farro piccolo*, is an ancient European grain related to wheat. Yes, it has gluten, but unlike common American wheat, spelt has not been subjected to the abuses of agribusiness, such as cross-breeding and genetic modification. Some sources believe that those intolerant of wheat may have an easier time digesting spelt and other ancient grains. Spelt is chewy, with a nutty, earthy flavor; it's great in salads, such as the Shaved Brussels Sprouts with Spelt, Walnuts, and Pecorino (page 98), spooned into soups, or served with yogurt or milk as a quick-and-easy breakfast cereal. Spelt takes more than an hour to cook, so if you're strapped for time, use wheat berries or farro, which take a bit less time, in its place. Soaking it for an hour or up to overnight before cooking will reduce the cooking time slightly. *Makes about 2 cups*

1 cup spelt, rinsed

2 teaspoons kosher salt

Bring 6 cups water to a boil in a medium saucepan over high heat. Add the spelt and salt. Reduce the heat to medium-high and gently boil the spelt, uncovered, until it is tender but still chewy, 60 to 70 minutes. Drain and serve, or transfer the spelt to a wide bowl or baking sheet to cool to room temperature if you are cooking it to use in a salad.

TEFF

Teff is a tiny ancient grain and a staple in Ethiopian cuisine; teff flour is used to make the Ethiopian bread *injera*. The grains, which come in brown and white (though brown is more common), are gluten-free and high in other nutrients, including iron. Some have dubbed teff the "new quinoa," but I'm not buying it. Where quinoa cooks up fluffy with a mild, easy-to-like flavor, teff is gummy, gluey, and has an unusual taste. I experimented a lot with teff before I found three ways to use it that were without a doubt as delicious as they were healthy. Teff is one of four grains in Four Grain "Nutella" Porridge (page 64). I use it to make a polenta-like base for Mole Teff and Chicken (page 174); and I used the miniscule grains as one might use polenta to make a Flourless Chocolate Teff Cake (page 218). It was only in retrospect that I realized all three uses contained chocolate, which complements or masks the vaguely chocolaty flavor of teff. I don't rinse teff before I cook it. It's too small. It would be like rinsing a poppy seed, and could only end in frustration.

WHEAT BERRIES

Wheat berries are just that: the whole kernels of wheat, including the bran, germ, and endosperm. Before farro and Khorasan wheat came back into our lives, wheat berries were the only grain of that type that you would see in a salad. I use them to make a Deconstructed Italian Easter Pie (page 224), wherein the berries, suspended in honey, are spooned over whipped goat cheese. And I stir leftover wheat berries into ricotta or yogurt for breakfast or dessert; I got this idea from an obscure Sicilian dessert that consists of cooked wheat berries stirred into a bowl of lightly sweetened ricotta and topped with shaved dark chocolate. I strongly suggest you cook yourself some wheat berries, pick up a tub of ricotta, and get on this right now. *Makes about 2 cups*

1 cup wheat berries, rinsed

2 teaspoons kosher salt

Bring 6 cups water to a boil in a medium saucepan over high heat. Add the wheat berries and salt. Reduce the heat to medium-high and gently boil the wheat berries, uncovered, until they are tender but still chewy, 50 to 60 minutes. Drain the wheat berries and serve, or transfer to a wide bowl or baking sheet to cool to room temperature if you're cooking them to use in a salad.

WILD RICE

Wild rice, an ancient cereal grain native to North America, is not actually rice—it's a grain variety all its own. It is high in protein, fiber, and other nutrients. When cooked properly (i.e., not *overcooked*), it is firm and chewy, and the long, slender grains keep their pretty, structured shape. It's a good gluten-free option in recipes calling for any of the gluten-containing grains, such as in the Shaved Brussels Sprouts with Spelt, Walnuts, and Pecorino (page 98) or the Farmers' Market Bowl (page 123). It is especially delicious with roasted vegetables and other foods with a fall or winter vibe. *Makes about 3 cups*

1 cup wild rice, rinsed

1 teaspoon kosher salt

Combine the wild rice, salt, and 2½ cups water in a large sauté pan over high heat. Bring the water to a boil, reduce the heat to low, cover the pan, and gently simmer until the grains are tender but not mushy, about 45 minutes. Turn off the heat and let the wild rice rest, covered, for 10 minutes. Uncover and fluff gently with a fork. Serve, or transfer the wild rice to a wide bowl or baking sheet to cool to room temperature if you're cooking it to use in a salad.

BOWLS
of
PLENTY

BREAKFAST BOWLS

I'm an early riser, and I can't start the day without breakfast. I'm also a rut eater, so what I'm eating today is probably what I'm going to eat tomorrow, and it's very possible I will eat the same thing the day after that. The ruts change from time to time. Oatmeal is my fallback rut, but, variety being the spice and all that, over the years I've made porridge of just about every grain imaginable. You'll find my most successful experiments here—and if you're not an early morning person, you'll be happy to know they can, each and every one of them, be made in advance. You'll also find savory breakfast options here: rice bowls with an egg on them, breakfast fried quinoa, and other delicious healthy meals. If you have cooked grains on hand, and I suggest you do, you can pull these breakfasts together in minutes. And remember these words: breakfast anytime.

GRANDMOTHER BIRDIE'S OATMEAL COCKTAIL with Raisins and Salty Sunflower Seeds 50

QUICK AND EASY BREAKFAST FRIED QUINOA 53

RICE BOWL WITH POACHED EGG, Slow-Roasted Tomatoes, and Feta 55

JAPANESE BREAKFAST with Spinach, Salmon, and Sweet Miso Dressing 61

FOUR GRAIN "NUTELLA" PORRIDGE with Toasted Hazelnuts and Jam 64

SLOW-COOKED BROWN RICE AND QUINOA PORRIDGE 68

ROSEMARY BUCKWHEAT CRUNCH with Fresh Ricotta 70

SPICED APPLE BREAKFAST FARRO with Yogurt Cream 72

PASTRAMI AND RYE BERRY HASH with Mustard Greens and Pickled Mustard Seeds 73

SWEET AND SALTY GRANOLA with Toasted Coconut and Pecans 75

ASIAN BREAKFAST PORRIDGE with Turkey Meatballs 76

COCONUT MILLET PORRIDGE with Bananas and Poppy Seeds 80

QUINOA HUEVOS RANCHEROS BOWL 83

GRANDMOTHER BIRDIE'S OATMEAL COCKTAIL
with Raisins and Salty Sunflower Seeds

2 cups milk (I like whole cow's milk here, but use what you like), plus more as needed

1 cinnamon stick, or 1 teaspoon ground cinnamon

1 teaspoon kosher salt

1 cup steel-cut oats

1 cup raisins, golden or black

4 tablespoons (½ stick) unsalted butter

¼ cup packed brown sugar

¼ cup hulled roasted salted sunflower seeds

Gray or pink (rock-like) sea salt or flaky sea salt, such as fleur de sel (optional)

My grandmother Birdie, whose oatmeal this is modeled after, was way ahead of her time in terms of women's liberation. For starters, she worked, when the vast majority of women didn't. And she didn't cook, except for one thing: oatmeal. She called her version "oatmeal cocktail," which made it feel special. And indeed it *was* special. Birdie stirred tons of brown sugar or honey into her oatmeal, and put a big plop of butter, which melted into glistening golden pools, on top. It was so sweet and decadent, it was like an oatmeal cookie in a bowl. But the best thing about that oatmeal was the salted sunflower seeds, which were strewn throughout like little crunchy salt vessels. I add even more salt, in the form of rock-like gray or pink salt, or flaky sea salt, at the end, because my love of sweet and salty knows no bounds.

When it comes to cooking oats in milk or water, I compromise: I use half milk, so the oatmeal turns out rich and creamy, and half water, just to cut the decadence quotient by half. Do what I do, or use all of one or the other. You could also use a dairy-free milk alternative. *Serves 4*

Combine the milk and 2 cups water in a medium saucepan. Add the cinnamon and kosher salt and bring the liquid to a boil over high heat. Stir in the oats and return the liquid to a boil. Reduce the heat to maintain a simmer and cook gently for 30 minutes, until the oats are tender. Add the raisins and simmer for 5 minutes more to plump them up. Fish out and discard the cinnamon stick if you used it.

Dish out the oatmeal into four bowls and add 1 tablespoon of butter to each dish while the oatmeal is piping hot. Sprinkle the brown sugar, sunflower seeds, and salt over the top, pour a little bit of cold milk around the edges of the bowl, and dig in.

COLD HOT CEREAL

When I make oatmeal, I always make enough for four, even if I only need one or two servings. I refrigerate the leftovers and then either reheat the cereal in a saucepan with a little water or milk, or, better yet, eat the cereal cold. Have you ever had cold hot cereal? I didn't think so. In the summer, I make hot oatmeal just so that I can refrigerate it and eat it cold. It's so delicious and so much healthier than any other, and I mean *any* other, cold cereal out there. If you're feeling fancy, toss some berries or dried fruit on top of your cold hot cereal, or cut up some soft in-season fruit, such as peaches, nectarines, or figs, and throw them on. Drizzle with honey, maple syrup, or agave syrup, scatter some kind of nuts or seeds over the top, and pour milk around the edges. You'll never cook a single serving of oatmeal again.

QUICK AND EASY
BREAKFAST FRIED QUINOA

4 thick slices bacon

1 bunch collard greens
(or kale or chard)

1 teaspoon kosher salt

3 cups cooked quinoa
(or brown rice; from 1 cup
uncooked grains, page 42
or 36)

4 eggs, lightly beaten

Sriracha

If I have a go-to breakfast, it's this fried quinoa, which can really be a fried any-grain. The grains and greens are cooked in the fat rendered from the bacon, so it's a one-dish wonder, and it takes about 15 minutes to make, including dishwashing time. I am not an indiscriminate Sriracha user, but the Sriracha scribbled on top really makes this breakfast.

To make it vegan, or if you simply aren't a bacon eater, don't add the bacon, and cook the scramble in olive or canola oil. This recipe is for four but it's something I throw together often when I'm feeding only myself. Just scale it down. *Serves 4*

Cook the bacon in a large (preferably nonstick) skillet over medium heat until the fat has rendered and the bacon is brown but not crispy, about 5 to 10 minutes, depending on the thickness of the bacon. Transfer the bacon to a bed of paper towels to cool; thinly slice crosswise.

Stack three or four collard leaves at a time and roll them lengthwise into a tight log. Cut across the log to thinly slice the leaves, stopping when you get to the stems, and discard the stems.

Increase the heat to medium-high, add the collards, and sprinkle with salt. Cook the greens for about 1 minute, folding

them with tongs so they cook evenly. Dump the quinoa into the pan, fold the grains in with the greens, and cook to warm the quinoa through. Lower the heat to medium-low and move the greens and grains to one side of the skillet to create space in the pan. Pour the eggs into the space you created in the pan and cook for about 1 minute until they look like soft scrambled eggs. Fold the greens and grains in with the eggs and turn off the heat. Add the bacon back to the pan and fold them in with the rest of the mess. Scribble Sriracha on top of the whole story, and serve with more Sriracha on the side.

RICE BOWL WITH POACHED EGG,
Slow-Roasted Tomatoes, and Feta

1 cup long-grain brown rice (or quinoa), cooked (see pages 36 and 42; about 3½ cups cooked grains)

4 poached eggs (see page 59)

8 halves of Slow-Roasted Tomatoes (recipe follows; or 8 sun-dried tomatoes, or 2 fresh in-season tomatoes, or 2 avocados, halved, pitted, and peeled)

2 to 3 ounces feta (¼ to ½ cup crumbled)

A big handful of fresh flat-leaf parsley and/or chives

Don't buy crumbled feta. Buy feta packed in water, which is available at any grocery store, and is infinitely creamier and moister than crumbled feta. How hard is it to crumble feta, I ask. Give it a whirl—you might even find that you enjoy touching your food.

Breakfast rice bowls such as this have taken over Los Angeles in the last half decade. People are *obsessed* with them. And for good reason: they're satisfying and healthy, and there's just something about spooning rice and runny eggs from a bowl and into your mouth that makes you feel all wrapped up and warm; it's like a free hug. The tomatoes called for here roast for hours to concentrate their sweetness, so if you haven't already made them or don't have several hours before hunger strikes, substitute sun-dried tomatoes or sliced fresh tomatoes. Looking for some variety in your life? Try the same toppings on a bowl of savory buckwheat breakfast porridge (see Buckwheat, page 37; or Millet Polenta, page 129). *Serves 4*

Mound the grains into four bowls. Slide one poached egg on each bowl and nestle the tomatoes beside it. Crumble the feta over the top and use scissors to snip the herbs over the bowl.

Slow-Roasted Tomatoes

Slow-roasted tomatoes are like tomato candy. Cooking them this way, in a warm oven for a long time, extracts the water from tomatoes, which concentrates their flavor; slow roasting can make even an average, out-of-season tomato taste pretty darned good. These tomatoes, leftover farro or wild rice, and a dollop of yogurt is my idea of a perfect healthy working lunch. I usually make a double batch so I have these delicious little gems to eat in various ways throughout the week. *Serves 4 to 6; makes 12 tomato halves*

6 Roma (plum) tomatoes, stemmed and halved lengthwise

6 garlic cloves, smashed

Handful of fresh thyme sprigs (6 to 10)

¼ cup olive oil

1 heaping teaspoon kosher salt

Adjust the oven racks so one is in the middle position and preheat the oven to 300°F.

Toss the tomatoes, garlic, thyme sprigs, olive oil, and salt in a medium baking dish (a pie dish works great for this). Turn the tomatoe halves cut-side up and roast until the tomatoes are browned and beginning to collapse, about 2 hours.

Let the tomatoes cool slightly before serving them. Store the tomatoes in a flat airtight container for up to 1 week and bring them to room temperature before serving.

EGGS EVERY WHICH WAY

My dad used to say that anybody could cook an egg, and I suppose anybody *can* cook an egg, if your criterion is simply "not raw." But in fact, eggs are one of the most difficult things to get right. Eggs are delicate. They're *eggs*. They're unformed matter waiting to be turned into greatness, either in the form of a chicken, or a perfectly cooked egg. This takes some finesse.

CRISPY FRIED EGGS

A properly fried egg, according to people who care about foods being made "properly" (i.e., the French), is one in which the white is cooked evenly from the yolk outward, so the resulting egg is completely without any gradations of color or texture: it looks like a cartoon drawing of an egg. This isn't how I like my fried eggs. I like my fried eggs with a thin, lacy, crispy edge around the outside of the white. Lucky for me, such an egg is much easier to achieve. I like to fry my eggs one at a time. They take only a couple of minutes to cook, and it's the only way I can be sure to get a crispy edge all the way around, rather than the whites bleeding together and my having to cut them apart.

To learn to fry eggs in the proper French manner, you'll have to go elsewhere. For a crisp, lacy-edged, olive oil–fried egg, read on.

Heat 1 tablespoon olive oil or butter in a small, nonstick skillet over medium-high heat until it's hot but not smoking, about 2 minutes. Crack 1 egg into the oil, sprinkle it with a pinch of salt and a few turns of pepper, and fry until the white is just set and the edges are golden brown, about 2 minutes for runny yolks, 2½ minutes for medium-cooked yolks.

POACHED EGGS

After boning up on fried eggs, poached eggs are a no-brainer. The delicate little glimmers in your hungry eyes are cooked in gently simmering water, not thrown violently into a hard pan of hot oil. The one trick to making poached eggs is to crack the eggs into a strainer; the wateriest part of the whites falls through the strainer, so the whites you're left with form a neat little package around the yolks. (All this to prevent the wispy whites that float away from the whites in the water; purely an aesthetic thing.)

To poach eggs without making it more difficult than it needs to be, fill a medium skillet 1 to 2 inches deep with water. Add a big glug of white vinegar and bring the liquid to a simmer over high heat. Reduce the heat until the water is quivering, but not bubbling. Gently crack one egg into a strainer and let whatever whites that want to drip out. Gently slide the egg from the strainer to the water. Wait 10 to 20 seconds so the egg has a chance to set, then repeat, adding a second, and then the third and fourth eggs, each time letting one egg set before adding another. Poach the eggs until the whites are set, 3 to 4 minutes. Using a slotted spoon or flat strainer, lift the eggs out of the water. Blot them on a paper towel or clean dishtowel before sending them on to their destined grain bowl, or wherever they are headed. Poached eggs, surprisingly, hold up really well. Store the poached eggs in a container with ice water, which stops the cooking process and keeps them moist. Drain them and heat them in simmering water for 30 seconds to warm through before serving.

BOILED EGGS

First, a glossary.

A *soft-boiled egg* is the sort of thing you eat for breakfast, with a spoon. You may spoon it straight out of the shell, or you can cut the shells open and scoop the eggs out of the shells into a bowl. To peel soft-boiled eggs, first make sure they're completely chilled, then gently crack them all over the surface of the egg and put them back in the ice bath for 5 to 10 minutes. Remove them and very gently peel.

A *medium-cooked egg* is one that has been cooked so the yolk has *just* solidified. In fact, the very center of the egg is still wet looking, but not so wet that it will drip. This is the perfect egg for adding to salads or to keep around the house to peel, salt, and snack on.

A *hard-boiled egg* is cooked all the way through. However, contrary to popular belief, hard-boiling eggs doesn't mean cooking the eggs in hot water while you wash the dishes, check your e-mails, and do a few downward dogs while you're at it because it doesn't really matter how long the eggs are cooked since they're going to be *hard boiled* anyway. Hard-boiled eggs should be boiled until they are cooked through, and not a nanosecond longer. The yolk on a properly hard-boiled egg is a uniform yellow throughout. There is no good reason for the gray ring around the yolk of a hard-boiled egg. An egg with a gray ring around the yolk is what I might call a "murdered egg."

I make hard-boiled eggs in three instances: when I am making egg salad; when I am making deviled eggs; and when I am making medium- or soft-cooked eggs and I forget to set a timer.

To make perfect soft-, medium-, or hard-boiled eggs: Start with one more egg than you want in the end. This is your testing and snacking egg. Fill a pot big enough to hold the number of eggs you are cooking with water and bring the water to a boil over high heat. Carefully add the eggs to the water without cracking them (I put a few eggs in a spider or strainer and lower them into the water). Cook the eggs (still over high heat) for 5 minutes. Turn off the heat and let the eggs sit in hot water for 4 minutes more for soft-boiled eggs; 5 minutes for medium-boiled eggs; and 6 minutes for hard-boiled eggs.

Meanwhile, fill a large bowl with a lot of ice and a little water. When your egg-cooking time is up, lift the eggs out of the hot water and put them in the ice bath to cool completely. Peel the eggs, pat them dry, and move on.

JAPANESE BREAKFAST
with Spinach, Salmon, and Sweet Miso Dressing

1 cup long-grain brown rice, rinsed and cooked (see page 36; 3½ cups cooked rice)

1 (10-ounce) clamshell prewashed spinach leaves (preferably baby spinach), lightly steamed

Poached Salmon (recipe follows)

Sweet Miso Dressing (recipe follows)

TOPPINGS

4 nori sheets, thinly sliced into threads, or furikake or toasted sesame seeds, for sprinkling

4 soft-boiled or medium-boiled eggs (optional; see page 59)

1 or 2 ripe avocados, pitted, peeled, and sliced (optional)

Pickled Vegetables (page 135; optional)

The best thing to happen for spinach since Popeye did his marketing of the vegetable can be summed up in a word: prewashed.

Years ago, I was staying at a fancy hotel in Las Vegas on a story assignment. When I went downstairs to breakfast, I noticed, across from the all-American breakfast buffet offering the usual artery clogging collection of greasy pork sausages, eggs, and every manner of white flour product slathered in butter and doused in butter, jam, or maple syrup, a Japanese breakfast buffet offering steamed rice, miso soup, salmon fillets and whole oily fish, pickles, and vegetables. Vegetables! For breakfast! I left old habits behind a piled up my plate with rice, spinach, and fish, and afterwards I felt so clear-headed and energized versions of that breakfast have been a favorite ever since. This is not a traditional Japanese breakfast, but the breakfast I make with a Japanese breakfast in mind, when I want to start my day with protein and vegetables, and feeling like a million yen.

The salmon I use here is poached and then refrigerated, which works for me because no matter how great I feel after eating fish for breakfast, I don't really want to *cook* fish for breakfast. Plus, with the fish already cooked, you can pull breakfast together in minutes. The only component that has to be piping hot is the rice, and the smell of steaming rice in the morning is almost as seductive as that of bacon, but in a very, *very* different way. *Serves 4*

Spoon the rice into four large bowls, or four smaller rice bowls if you're serving bento box style. Sprinkle the rice with the nori threads. Pile the spinach on top of the rice (or in a separate dish if you're going bento) and drizzle with the sweet miso dressing. If you are adding any of the optional components, add them to the bowl on, or put them in separate dishes around, the rice. Serve with the remaining miso dressing on the side for drizzling.

recipe continues

Poached Salmon

I tend to like big, robust flavors, so I was late to try poached fish. Boy was I missing out. In fact, poached fish is so ridiculously delicious that I always poach more than I need so I have enough for the next day, and the next. And it's so easy to make and foolproof. I made many of the poaching ingredients in this recipe optional; make it with what you have. *Makes 1 pound*

OPTIONAL POACHING INGREDIENTS

1 Spanish yellow onion, peeled and halved

1 carrot, broken in half

1 celery stalk, broken in half

A small handful of parsley sprigs

1 bay leaf (preferably fresh)

1 teaspoon whole black peppercorns

½ cup white wine

1 arbol chile pod (or a pinch of red pepper flakes)

2 lemons, halved

1 (1-pound) skin-on salmon fillet

Choose a deep straight-sided skillet that is large enough to fit the salmon fillet in one layer. Put the poaching ingredients that you are using into the skillet. Squeeze the lemon juice into the pan and drop the lemon halves into the pan. Add 6 cups water and bring the liquid to a boil over high heat. Reduce the heat to maintain a simmer and cook for about 20 minutes to infuse the water with the poaching ingredients.

Lay the salmon skin-side down in the pan; move the poaching veggies around (or remove and toss them) to make room for the salmon. If the salmon isn't covered in liquid, add enough water so it is barely covered. Return the water to a simmer. Gently simmer—you want the water barely bubbling; reduce the heat if it's boiling—until the salmon is just cooked through, 8 to 12 minutes. To test for doneness, gently separate the fish with a fork or your fingers; if it pulls apart easily and is opaque throughout, it's done. If not, give it another minute or two and test it again.

Remove the salmon from the liquid and use your fingers to gently pull back, remove, and discard the skin. Serve it hot, or transfer to a plate and let it cool to room temperature. If you're cooking the fish to eat later, after it cools to room temperature, wrap it in plastic wrap and refrigerate for up to 2 days.

Sweet Miso Dressing

Makes about ¼ cup

¼ cup sweet white miso

¼ cup rice vinegar

2 tablespoons mirin (Japanese sweet rice wine; substitute dry sherry)

1 tablespoon sugar

1 teaspoon low-sodium soy sauce or tamari

1 teaspoon kosher salt

Whisk all the ingredients together in a small bowl until the dressing is smooth. It will keep, refrigerated in a covered container, for weeks.

FOUR GRAIN "NUTELLA" PORRIDGE
with Toasted Hazelnuts and Jam

¼ cup millet, rinsed

¼ cup quinoa, rinsed

¼ cup amaranth

¼ cup teff

4 cups hazelnut milk, homemade, see Homemade Nut Milk (page 65) or store-bought, plus more for serving

1½ teaspoons kosher salt

2 ounces bittersweet or semisweet chocolate, cut into small pieces (about ½ cup)

1 cup hazelnuts, toasted (see page 69)

1 tablespoon hazelnut oil or extra-virgin olive oil

¼ cup raspberry jam

I want to go on the record that I don't think chocolate for breakfast is particularly healthy, but if you *are* going to have chocolate for breakfast, working it into this super-grain porridge is a good way to go. The grains are cooked with hazelnut milk, so it's like Nutella, minus the palm oil and the bread you smear the Nutella on. If you don't have all four grains on hand, use whatever combination of grains you like, as long as you start with 1 cup uncooked grains. *Serves 4*

Combine the millet, quinoa, amaranth, and teff in a medium saucepan. Add the milk and 1 teaspoon of the salt and bring to a boil over medium-high heat. Reduce the heat to low and simmer until the grains are tender, 20 to 25 minutes. Turn off the heat and stir in the chocolate.

Put the toasted hazelnuts on a cutting board; run a knife through them once or twice to coarsely chop, then put the nuts in a small bowl. Toss with the oil and the remaining ½ teaspoon salt.

To serve, ladle the porridge into four individual bowls. Spoon 1 tablespoon of jam onto each serving and sprinkle with the hazelnuts. Serve with additional milk on the side.

HOMEMADE NUT MILK

I seriously thought I would knit my own socks before I would make my own nut milk. It just seemed like a lot of work for little payoff. But as is so often the case, I was wrong. In fact, making nut milk is not much work at all: soak, drain, blend, strain, drink, repeat. And indeed, the payoff is significant. Homemade nut milk is creamy, flavorful, and refreshing. Even the color is a nice, warm white like you'd use to paint exposed brick walls, as opposed to the drab, dirty, institutional gray-white shade of store-bought nut milk. And in any pursuit of optimum deliciousness, I blend a whole or half vanilla bean pod into my nut milk, a trick I learned from my friend Adriene Hughes. The fact that I throw the entire pod into the blender makes me feel better about the money I spent on that pod. I've tried milking every kind of nut there is to milk and I'll just stop here to say, there's a reason almond milk is the most popular of the nut milks. It has the mildest flavor of them all, and is also the creamiest. Cashew milk and milk made from Brazil nuts are both super rich; and hazelnut milk is terrific, if you're looking for the taste of hazelnuts—because it has a very intense flavor.

A nut milk bag, which you can buy at some health food and housewares stores, makes easy work of straining and squeezing every last drop from the ground nuts, but if you don't have one, you can get by with a fine mesh strainer or large coffee filter.

Note that you will need to double this recipe to make enough nut milk for cooking and serving the Four Grain "Nutella" Porridge (page 64). *Makes about 3½ cups*

1 cup raw almonds, hazelnuts, or cashews, soaked overnight or for at least 6 hours

1 whole or half vanilla bean, halved crosswise, not down the middle (optional)

Pinch of kosher salt

4 cups filtered water

1 tablespoon agave syrup (optional)

Put the nuts in a bowl of water; add the vanilla bean, if you are using it, and soak overnight or for at least several hours. Drain and discard the soaking water. Transfer the nuts and vanilla, if you used it, to a blender, add the salt, filtered water, and agave, if you're using it, and puree.

Pour the milk into a nut milk bag or strain it through a fine-mesh strainer (no cheesecloth necessary) or a coffee filter and press down on the nut meal to extract as much milk as possible. Discard the nut meal. Put the milk in a couple of big jars or containers with lids, so you can give it a shake before you pour. It will keep in the refrigerator for up to several days.

SLOW-COOKED BROWN RICE AND QUINOA PORRIDGE

½ cup long- or short-grain brown rice, rinsed

½ cup white quinoa, rinsed

3 cups milk (or almond milk), plus more for serving

¼ cup organic sugar (or turbinado or granulated sugar)

¼ teaspoon kosher salt

Quality fruit jam

Fresh seasonal fruit (such as figs, blueberries, peaches, nectarines)

Almonds, hazelnuts, walnuts, or pecans, toasted (see page 69)

There's a café in Los Angeles called Sqirl that serves a milky rice porridge topped with jam and chopped nuts, both of which—the restaurant and the porridge—have an almost cult-like following. I had been making brown rice breakfast cereal for over a decade using brown rice milled into the texture of Cream of Wheat, but I got the idea from Squirl to cook the whole grains until they completely lose their shape. I use a mix of rice and quinoa, but you can make it with all rice or all quinoa.

This is not a last-minute breakfast, as you cook the grains for over an hour. You can, however, make a big batch on a lazy Sunday (assuming people still have those), and heat it up throughout the week. *Serves 4*

Combine the rice, quinoa, milk, sugar, salt, and 3 cups water in a medium saucepan over medium heat. When the liquid starts bubbling around the edges, reduce the heat to maintain a gentle simmer and cook the grains, stirring occasionally so they don't stick to the bottom of the pot and a skin doesn't form on the top, until the rice is completely broken down and shapeless and the porridge is a soupy consistency, about 1 hour (the quinoa tends to maintain its shape). If the liquid is almost completely cooked off but you feel the grains could be cooked more, add more water and keep cooking. Serve hot, topped with the jam, the fruit, and nuts of your choice, and more milk.

PB&J PORRIDGE

I got the idea to apply the winning, all-American combo of PB&J to whole-grain porridge from a book in which the author talked about the peanut butter porridge his mom made him back home in Senegal. Yes, Senegal. And here I thought Americans invented peanut butter. To make PB&J porridge, eliminate the add-ins (fruit, nuts, spices) from any porridge (except one made with coconut milk) and stir ½ cup peanut butter (or the nut butter of your choice) into the finished porridge. Top with a handful of chopped, roasted nuts to match the butter and a spoonful of fruit jam. Easy as toast. And a lot healthier.

TOASTING NUTS

No skilled home cook or chef worth his sea salt would ever throw nuts into a dish without toasting them first. When nuts are toasted, they go from a healthy snack to a crunchy, flavorful addition to a dish. Toasting takes so little time, and it doesn't just bring out the flavor of the nut, it changes the flavor—for the better. Plus, toasted nuts are crunchier, and who doesn't love crunch? The bottom line: Toast your nuts.

If you want to take your nuts to the next level, after toasting them, toss them in oil and season them with sea salt before eating them or adding them to a dish. Extra-virgin olive oil will highlight the flavor (not to mention the unique, bark-like color and texture) of any nut, but if you have them, toss walnuts in walnut oil and hazelnuts in hazelnut oil. I don't recommend toasting nuts in a skillet on the stovetop. They don't toast throughout, and more often than not, the exterior burns. Toast nuts in the oven. Here's how:

Adjust the oven racks so one is in the middle position and preheat the oven to 325°F. Scatter the nuts on a baking sheet and toast them in the oven, shaking the pan once or twice so they toast all over and don't burn. You'll know they're done when they've browned slightly and when you can smell the aroma of the nuts wafting from the oven.

Below is a rough estimate on times:

Almonds and Hazelnuts: 12 to 15 minutes

Walnuts and Pecans: 10 to 12 minutes

Pine Nuts and Pepitas (Pumpkin Seeds): 8 to 10 minutes

Hazelnuts require one more step: you have to remove the skins after toasting them. To do this, after toasting the nuts, put them in a clean dishtowel, close the dishtowel to create a bundle, and roll the nuts around inside the towel. When you open up the bundle, the nuts will no longer be wearing their skins. Shake the skins out of the towel and send the nuts on to their destiny.

No matter how strongly you believe that you will remember something in the oven, on the stove, or in the freezer for just a few minutes, one of these times, you will forget, and your dinner or cookies or nuts will be ruined. Set a timer. The pros rely on timers. Why shouldn't you?

ROSEMARY BUCKWHEAT CRUNCH
with Fresh Ricotta

FOR THE CRUNCH

1 cup buckwheat

1 cup walnut halves

2 tablespoons canola oil or another neutral-flavored oil

2 tablespoons pure maple syrup

½ teaspoon kosher salt

¼ cup fresh rosemary

FOR THE BOWLS

8 ounces good-quality store-bought ricotta (preferably sheep's-milk ricotta, or plain sheep's- or goat's-milk yogurt)

Honey (preferably buckwheat or chestnut honey), for drizzling

I first tasted ricotta on its own, as opposed to a layer in lasagna, at lunch with Colman Andrews, one of the founding editors of *Saveur* magazine and my friend and mentor in food writing. We were at Mario Batali's Lupa Trattoria in Greenwich Village, and for dessert, the restaurant sent him a plate of sheep's-milk ricotta drizzled with chestnut honey, a dark-colored honey with a funky, woody, slightly bitter flavor. The combination of cheese and chestnut honey, Colman told me, is an Italian classic. I reached over, took a bite, and about fell out of my chair. Two ingredients. Cheese. And honey. And yet so completely out of this world. I add toasted buckwheat and walnuts for crunch and nutrition, so I can call it "breakfast." The crunch topping also makes a delicious breakfast cereal served over yogurt or with milk. It's like nature's Grape Nuts. *Serves 4*

Preheat the oven to 325°F.

To make the crunch, toss the buckwheat, walnuts, oil, maple syrup, and salt on a baking sheet and spread the ingredients out in an even layer. Bake for 15 minutes, until the buckwheat is barely golden. Shake the pan or stir the buckwheat so it browns evenly. Remove from the oven, stir in the rosemary, and return the baking sheet to the oven until the buckwheat is golden brown and the rosemary is crispy but not burnt, about 5 minutes. Remove from the oven and set aside for the buckwheat to cool to room temperature and crisp up.

To serve the bowls, spoon the ricotta into four small bowls, dividing it evenly. Drizzle with honey and sprinkle with the crunch topping.

SPICED APPLE BREAKFAST FARRO
with Yogurt Cream

FOR THE FARRO

2 apples

5 to 10 whole cloves, or
a pinch of ground cloves
(optional)

6 cups fresh apple cider or
apple juice (the cloudier
the juice, the better), plus
more as needed

1 cinnamon stick, or ½
teaspoon ground cinnamon,
plus more for sprinkling

¼ teaspoon kosher salt

1½ cups farro, rinsed

Yogurt Cream (recipe
follows)

*G-Free Alternative: To make
this recipe gluten-free, make it
with whole oat groats instead
of farro.*

For many years while I was trying to make ends meet as a writer, I worked selling fruit for a seventh-generation Hudson Valley farmer at the Union Square Greenmarket in New York City. Working there, I made less money per hour than a slice of pie would have cost at the corner diner (this being New York City), but I had all the apples a girl could wish for. I made applesauce, apple crisps, apple cake, apple butter, apple slaw, apple soup. (Yes, apple soup. Did I mention I was cash broke and apple rich?) And I got creative with the apple cider in recipes like this hot cereal. It's so sweet and delicious that you won't even want to add sugar. I top it with a mix of yogurt and sour cream, which takes an otherwise dairy-free breakfast *out* of the dairy-free category, so if dairy-free is a priority, serve it with nut or grain milk, or warm cider instead. *Serves 4*

Peel the apples and cut each one into four slabs around the core, removing the core in one piece. If you're using whole cloves, stud the cloves into one of the apple cores (throw out the other core). Thinly slice the apple slabs.

Put the apple cider, cinnamon stick, clove-studded apple core (or ground cinnamon and cloves), and salt in a medium saucepan. Bring the cider to a boil over high heat. Add the farro, reduce the heat slightly, and gently boil until the farro is tender, 15 to 20 minutes. Add the sliced apples and cook for 5 minutes so they soften but not so long that they turn into applesauce. Remove and discard the apple core and cinnamon stick, if you used them.

Spoon the farro into four bowls, dollop the cream on top, on each bowl, arrange the apples on top, sprinkle with cinnamon, and serve.

Yogurt Cream

This isn't really a recipe: It's yogurt mixed with sour cream and, if you're feeling sweet, a spoonful of sugar. It's a clear example of the sum being greater than the parts. Dollop this wonderful concoction on sweet breakfast or dessert. *Makes 2 cups*

1 cup plain yogurt

1 cup sour cream

1 teaspoon sugar (or whatever sweetener you like; optional)

Stir all the ingredients together in a small bowl. The cream will last for 1 week, refrigerated.

PASTRAMI AND RYE BERRY HASH
with Mustard Greens and Pickled Mustard Seeds

Olive oil

4 ounces sliced pastrami, chopped (or 4 slices bacon, chopped)

1 bunch mustard greens, kale, collard greens, or Swiss chard, stemmed, leaves torn into bite-size pieces

1 teaspoon kosher salt

1 cup cooked rye berries (see page 43; or another chewy grain such as farro or wheat berries)

2 tablespoons Pickled Mustard Seeds (recipe follows), plus more for serving

4 fried eggs (see page 58)

G-Free Alternative: Using wild rice or sorghum in place of the rye berries in this recipe will make this gluten-free.

When I was in college at U.C. Berkeley, I worked as a waitress in a Jewish deli across the bay in San Francisco, where I discovered the unsung combination of pastrami and eggs. I add mustard greens and rye berries to the bowl as a wink to pastrami on rye, but you could use any chewy, hearty grain you want. Mustard greens are spicy and slightly bitter, but the pickled mustard seeds, which are sweet, take care of that potential problem. You can use kale, collard greens, beet greens, or chard in place of the mustard greens. *Serves 4*

Pour enough olive oil to coat a large skillet (preferably nonstick) and heat over medium-high heat until the oil is sizzling hot but not smoking, 2 to 3 minutes. Add the pastrami and cook, stirring to cook evenly, until it is golden brown and crispy in places, about 2 minutes. Add the greens, sprinkle with the salt, and cook for about 2 minutes, until they are just wilted, folding the greens so they cook evenly. Turn off the heat and fold in the rye berries and mustard seeds. Spoon the hash into four bowls and put them near the stove while you fry the eggs.

Remove the eggs as they are done and set one on each bowl. Top each bowl with a spoonful of the pickled mustard seeds and serve the rest on the side.

WARMING OIL

When warming oil in a pan, tilt the pan and watch how the oil changes. When oil is hot enough to sear, it will slide like water in the pan. You may also notice little streaks in the oil in the pan, like "legs" running down the side of a glass of red wine. This means your oil is ready. If the oil gets so hot that the pan begins to smoke, it's burnt. You have to start over. Don't let the oil smoke.

Pickled Mustard Seeds

I discovered pickled mustard seeds when I tested a recipe for them for the cookbook *Mozza at Home*. I was a little intimidated by the idea, not being much of a pickler myself, and never having used mustard seeds in my life to that point. But this is how easy they are to make: Boil water, pour it over mustard seeds (which, by the way are readily available in the spice section of supermarkets, health food stores, and Mexican, Indian, and Middle Eastern markets), the end. The seeds are slightly sweet and very mustardy, and when you bite into one, you get this great little pop like you do when biting into tobiko (flying fish eggs) in a sushi roll. Being that they are pickled, they last somewhere near forever, so now I keep a jar of them in my refrigerator to spoon into egg salad, or onto any bowl where mustard wouldn't be a bad idea. *Makes about 1¼ cups*

¼ cup yellow or black mustard seeds

½ cup apple cider vinegar

2 teaspoons honey

1 bay leaf

1 teaspoon kosher salt

Put the mustard seeds in a pint-size canning jar with a lid or in a heatproof medium bowl.

Combine the vinegar, honey, bay leaf, and salt in a small saucepan and bring the liquid to a boil over high heat. Turn off the heat and pour the boiling liquid over the mustard seeds. Set aside to cool to room temperature.

Put the lid on the jar or cover the bowl tightly with plastic wrap and set the mustard seeds aside for 2 to 3 hours, until the pickling liquid has saturated the seeds (the finished condiment will look like a seedy syrup) and they pop like caviar in your mouth. Use the seeds or put the lid on the jar (or transfer to another covered container) and refrigerate for up to several months.

SWEET AND SALTY GRANOLA
with Toasted Coconut and Pecans

½ cup melted butter (or olive oil or coconut oil)

⅓ cup pure maple syrup

¼ cup packed light or dark brown sugar

1 teaspoon ground cinnamon

1 teaspoon chili powder

2 teaspoons kosher salt

4 cups rolled oats

1 heaping cup cornflakes (or bran flakes)

1½ cups coarsely chopped pecans (or pepitas)

1 cup unsweetened large-flake coconut

Not long ago I was making granola when a friend texted, asking me what I was doing. It was eight thirty AM on a chilly (for San Diego) morning and he was texting from the fifth tee of a nine-hole golf course. "Why are you making granola?" he asked. "Don't they sell that stuff?" I asked him why he didn't play Nintendo Wii golf, sparing himself the drive and the cold and the whole hassle of leaving the house. He text-laughed.

The fact that you can buy granola and that, these days, living in the foodie nation that we do, you can buy some really *good* granola and maybe even have that granola delivered to your doorstep, misses the point. Of course you can buy granola! Or you could put *Astral Weeks* on the stereo, open your cupboards, pull down the oats canister and a few other goodies, get out your biggest mixing bowl, and in a few short minutes, enjoy the sweet, buttery scent wafting through a warm house, relishing in your morning accomplishment. Next, make sure to send a picture of said granola to as many people as possible, or post it on social media. If you do something simple and earnest before seven AM, don't you think the world should know?

Makes about 6 cups

Adjust the oven racks so one is in the upper third and the other in the lower third and preheat the oven to 350°F.

Combine the butter, maple syrup, brown sugar, cinnamon, chili powder, and salt in a big bowl and stir to distribute the salt and spices. Add the oats, cornflakes, and pecans and use a rubber spatula to fold the cereal ingredients and coat them with the flavorful goop in the bottom of the bowl.

Spread the granola out over two large baking sheets in an even layer and bake for 20 minutes, stirring once or twice during cooking and rotating the baking sheets from one rack to the other so the granola browns evenly and the bits around the edges don't burn. Remove the baking sheets from the oven, add the coconut, and return the granola to the oven to toast until the coconut and oats are golden brown, about 4 minutes.

Remove the baking sheets from the oven and let the granola cool to room temperature. Pack the granola in airtight containers. It will keep for at least a week, or longer, if you are able to resist finishing it off.

ASIAN BREAKFAST PORRIDGE
with Turkey Meatballs

FOR THE PORRIDGE

4 cups chicken stock, homemade (page 79) or sodium-free or low-sodium store-bought

½ cup long-grain brown rice, rinsed

½ teaspoon kosher salt

FOR THE MEATBALLS

½ pound ground dark meat turkey

1 tablespoon finely chopped fresh cilantro

1 tablespoon low-sodium soy sauce or tamari

1 teaspoon Worcestershire sauce (optional; use it if you have it)

2 garlic cloves, grated on a Microplane or minced

1 (1½-inch) piece fresh ginger, peeled and grated on a Microplane or minced

½ teaspoon kosher salt

FOR THE BOWLS

4 poached eggs (see page 59)

2 scallions, white and light green parts only, thinly sliced on an angle

1 (1-inch) piece fresh ginger, peeled and cut into matchsticks

Low-sodium soy sauce or tamari, for serving

The idea of eating Asian food for breakfast can be hard for some to wrap their minds around even if, as the clever people in your life will tell you, Asians do it every day. Asian rice porridge such as this is called congee. It's warm, soothing, and easy to love. The rice takes forever and a day (or about 2 hours) to cook so make it when you have time to spare, or cook it in advance and reheat it. You can skip the meatballs—there's enough going on with the ginger, scallions, poached egg, and soy sauce that your porridge won't be sad. It *will*, however, lose some of its personality if it's made with vegetable stock or water instead of chicken stock. *Serves 4*

To make the porridge, combine the stock, rice, and salt in a large saucepan and bring the liquid to a boil over high heat. Reduce the heat to low and very gently simmer for 40 minutes to 1 hour, until the rice has absorbed the stock, but not so long that the rice is dry. Add 1 cup of water and cook the rice, adding 1 cup more water at a time, until it is completely broken down and shapeless and the porridge is a loose, soupy consistency, about 1½ hours; you will add a total of 7 to 8 cups water.

Meanwhile, to make the meatballs, put the turkey in a medium bowl. Add the rest of the meatball ingredients and gently knead the meat to distribute the ingredients.

Roll the meat into 1-tablespoon-size balls and put the balls on a plate. Cover and refrigerate the meatballs for at least 30 minutes and up to overnight. (This isn't crucial, but it does help prevent the balls from falling apart when they're cooked. It's also a handy make-ahead trick.)

When the porridge is done, gently drop the balls into the porridge and cook over low heat for about 5 minutes until they're cooked through, gently rolling them to cook them on all sides. The only way to test the meatballs for doneness is to take one out and break it open; if it's pink, keep cooking.

Spoon the porridge and three or four meatballs into individual bowls. Put one poached egg on each bowl of porridge. Scatter the scallions and ginger on top, drizzle soy sauce around the edges of the bowl, and serve with more soy sauce on the side.

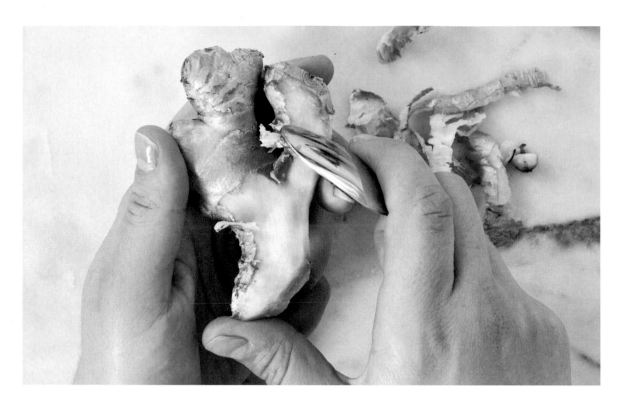

The easiest way to peel ginger is by scraping the skin off with the edge of a spoon.

CHICKEN STOCK

I make this basic chicken stock every few weeks and store it in quart containers in the refrigerator and freezer. It doesn't have any salt in it, which makes it easier to control how much salt I add to a recipe. If you don't want to make your own stock, buy sodium-free or low-sodium stock, and look for stock that doesn't contain MSG (monosodium glutamate) or maltodextrin. If you use store-bought stock that contains sodium, hold back on the salt in recipes that call for stock. *Makes 4 quarts or more*

---

5 pounds chicken bones (feet, backs, or other bones intended for stock)

1 large Spanish yellow onion, peeled, root end trimmed and discarded, and quartered

1 large carrot, cut into a few segments

1 celery stalk, cut into a few segments

1 tablespoon whole black peppercorns

Put the chicken bones in a tall stockpot with an insert, if you have one, or else in any large pot. Fill the pot with enough water to cover the bones by several inches and bring the water to a boil over high heat. Reduce the heat and gently boil the chicken bones, skimming the gray foam that rises to the top, until the stock stops foaming. Add the onion, carrot, celery, and peppercorns. Reduce the heat to maintain a simmer and cook for 2 to 2½ hours, until the stock is light golden. Turn off the heat and lift out the pot insert, if you used one, or pour the stock through a fine-mesh strainer set over another vessel that's big enough to catch the stock. Press on the bones and veggies to extract as much of the flavorful liquid as you can. Discard the solids and set aside stock to cool to room temperature. Scrape off any fat that forms on top. Refrigerate the stock for up to several days or freeze for months.

COCONUT MILLET PORRIDGE
with Bananas and Poppy Seeds

1 (15-ounce) can coconut milk, shaken

1 teaspoon ground cardamom (optional; use it if you have it)

¾ teaspoon kosher salt

1 cup millet, rinsed

2 ripe bananas

1 teaspoon poppy seeds, flaxseeds, or hemp seeds, or all of the above

1 cup unsweetened large-flake coconut

Cold coconut milk for serving

One of the things I love about this porridge is that it's sugar-free, dairy-free, and gluten-free, and all by accident. It was born that way. The first time I made it, I just set out to create a delicious alternative to oatmeal, not because I have anything against oatmeal, but because, well, even my dog likes a little variety in his morning diet. It was only later that I realized it was also so virtuous. If you really want to treat yourself special, forget the sliced banana and top this with pan-seared bananas or pineapple (see Pan-Seared Fruit, page 233).

In recent years I've started seeing coconut milk for sale in cartons, along with other alternative milks in the refrigerated dairy case at grocery stores. This coconut milk isn't as rich as the stuff in cans. I use canned coconut milk to make the porridge and refrigerated coconut milk *on* the porridge. Use what you want. *Serves 4*

Pour the coconut milk into a saucepan. Fill the empty coconut milk can with water and add the water to the saucepan and bring the liquid to a boil over high heat. Stir in the cardamom (if you're using it), salt, and millet, reduce the heat to maintain a simmer, and cook, stirring often, until the millet is tender but not mushy and the liquid has been absorbed, about 30 minutes.

Adjust the oven racks so one is in the middle position and preheat the oven to 325°F. Scatter the coconut on a baking sheet and toast in the oven for about 8 minutes, until it is light brown and fragrant, shaking the pan once or twice so the coconut doesn't burn.

Spoon the porridge into four bowls. Peel the bananas and slice them over the bowls so the slices fall onto the bowls. Sprinkle the poppy seeds and toasted coconut on top and serve with coconut milk around the edges.

QUINOA HUEVOS RANCHEROS BOWL

1 cup quinoa, cooked (see page 42; about 3½ cups cooked quinoa; or Corn Rice or Quinoa, Mexican Restaurant Rice, or Poblano Rice page 200, 195, or 180)

1½ to 2 cups cooked black beans (recipe follows) or 1 (15-ounce) can, warmed in their canning liquid

2 avocados, halved, pitted, peeled, and thinly sliced

1 lime, halved

Kosher salt and freshly ground black pepper

4 eggs, cooked in whatever way you like (see page 58)

Tomatillo salsa (store-bought; or Smoky Tomato Salsa, page 193)

½ cup Mexican crema, for drizzling (or sour cream thinned with milk or water to a drizzling consistency)

½ cup crumbled queso cotija, queso fresco, or feta

Handful of fresh cilantro leaves

If you ask me, Mexican breakfast = best breakfast. And since I always have black beans and salsa in the house—homemade or store-bought—this Mexican breakfast bowl has the added advantage of being a totally attainable breakfast goal.

Queso cotija is aged Mexican cheese, similar in texture to Parmesan. *Queso fresco* is a fresh, white Mexican cheese. You can find both cheeses at many standard grocery stores or use feta instead. *Serves 4*

Spoon the quinoa and beans side by side into four bowls and lay the avocado slices on top. Squeeze lime juice over the avocados and season them with salt and pepper.

Put the bowls by the stove while you cook the eggs to your heart's desire.

Put one egg on each bowl. Spoon salsa around the eggs and garnish the whole bowl with a drizzle of cream, a sprinkling of cheese, and a scattering of cilantro.

recipe continues

Black Beans

Simple, delicious black beans are a key part of any healthy, bowl-loving lifestyle. Canned beans are pretty good, and I always have some for making last-minute meals. But I also like to make my own; it's less expensive, and homemade beans are just a whole lot more flavorful The beans will keep in the refrigerator for up to 5 days. You can also freeze the beans in their cooking liquid.

Makes about 2 quarts

1 pound black beans, soaked overnight and drained

1 Spanish yellow onion, peeled and halved horizontally

1 head garlic, halved crosswise

1 bay leaf (preferably fresh; optional)

1 árbol chile (or a pinch of red pepper flakes; optional)

1 tablespoon kosher salt

Put the beans in a large pot. Add the onion, garlic, and bay leaf and chile, if you're using them. Add enough water to cover the beans by 2 inches. Bring the water to a boil over high heat, reduce the heat to maintain a simmer, and cook until the beans are tender and not the least bit chalky in the middle, about 1 hour, adding more water as necessary to keep them covered by an inch or two. Turn off the heat, stir in the salt, and let the beans rest for 20 minutes to absorb the salt. Add more water if the beans drank it all up while they rested. Remove the garlic and squeeze the cloves out of the head into the beans; discard the garlic skins. You can remove the other vegetables or just serve around them; I do the latter.

PUT AN AVOCADO ON IT!

Having grown up in San Diego, the avocado-growing capital of the country, with 13 avocado trees in my own backyard, I can attest to the fact that there is avocado life beyond the beloved, buttery Hass. There are seven varieties grown commercially in the United States, including those I picked from my own backyard trees, Fuerte, which are longer and narrower than Hass, with shiny green skins. Hass, which represent 95 percent of the avocados sold in America today, have a consistent creamy texture and delicious flavor, but if you happen upon a different variety of avocado, indulge your sense of adventure. Buy one, bring it home, and eat it.

Until recently, my method of getting an avocado out of its skin has been to scoop the flesh out with a big spoon. This does the job, but it doesn't always look terrific. Since you are probably going to want to take a picture of your avocado-dressed grain bowl and post it on Instagram (wink), I am going to tell you how to make your avocado look pretty.

First, cut the avocado in half. Give both halves a gentle twist to separate them. You will now have an avocado half in each hand. Put the halves down on a cutting board and gently but with authority plunge the side of your knife blade into the pit. Give the knife a twist to release the pit, which your knife is now married to. To release the pit and the blade from this bond, knock the pit against the cutting board. Now put your avocado halves cut-side down. Find an edge of the peel that you can lift up with your fingers and gently pull on it with the hope of lifting it all in one piece. Sometimes this works, other times the peel breaks off in pieces, but at least you tried.

Salt is key to the flavor of an avocado. I never add avocado to anything—not to a hamburger, not to a salad, not to a grain bowl, and not to my mouth—without salting it first. I might also squeeze some lime or lemon juice on it and drizzle it with oil before I salt it, and I might also grind pepper over it. But I always, always salt it.

SALAD BOWLS

Maybe it's my California roots or my salad-obsessed mother, but I could live on salad. These bowls are tossed rather than the ingredients arranged like a pie chart in the current grain-bowl style, because I want to make sure the dressing coats every last particle in the salad. These are the ideal bowls to take to work or to a picnic or potluck, because they're all dressed and ready to go, meant to be served at room temperature, and, because they're made with crunchy veggies like cabbage, broccolini, and carrots, they don't wilt over time. So get ready to welcome grain salads into your life and say goodbye to the sad desk lunch.

QUINOA AND POACHED SALMON SALAD with Confetti Vegetables 90

RAINBOW CARROT SALAD with Millet, Feta, and Lemon Yogurt Dressing 93

ITALIAN ANTIPASTO RICE SALAD with Tuna and Egg 95

RED BEET AND QUINOA SALAD with Hazelnuts and Goat Cheese 96

SHAVED BRUSSELS SPROUTS with Spelt, Walnuts, and Pecorino 98

SESAME DUCK AND WILD RICE SALAD 100

UMBRIAN FARRO AND BEAN SALAD with Celery Leaf Pesto and Mozzarella 103

SORGHUM GREEK SALAD 105

WINTER WILD RICE SALAD with Dates and Parmesan 106

CHINESE CHICKEN SALAD with Toasted Almonds and Crispy Rice 109

BROCCOLINI AND SPROUT SALAD with Poppy Seed Dressing and Avocado 111

QUINOA AND POACHED SALMON SALAD
with Confetti Vegetables

1 cup quinoa, cooked and cooled to room temperature (see page 42; about 3½ cups cooked quinoa)

1 bunch radishes, trimmed, scrubbed, and diced very small

½ red onion, diced very small

1 small fennel bulb, quartered, cored, and diced very small

2 celery stalks, diced very small

Lemon Vinaigrette (recipe follows)

12 ounces Poached Salmon (page 63), at room temperature or chilled

¼ cup fresh dill sprigs

This refreshing quinoa salad is my idea of spa cuisine. The quinoa is tossed with crunchy veggies including celery, fennel, and radishes, chopped really small like confetti, a light, lemon vinaigrette, and poached salmon flaked on the top. I love a dish like this, which is healthy not because I tried to make it so, or made compromises. It just is. If you want to decorate with pretty radish rounds, reserve two radishes, thinly slice them on a mandoline, and scatter them over the top of the finished salads. *Serves 4 to 6*

Put the quinoa, radishes, onion, fennel, and celery in a large bowl. Drizzle with the vinaigrette and gently toss to combine with a rubber spatula. Gently flake the salmon into large chunks, letting them fall into the bowl with the quinoa and scatter the dill and sliced radishes (if you're using them) over the top.

Lemon Vinaigrette

Makes about ¾ cup

1 medium shallot, minced

1 tablespoon champagne vinegar or white wine vinegar

Juice of 1 lemon

1 tablespoon kosher salt

Freshly ground black pepper

½ cup extra-virgin olive oil

Combine the shallot, vinegar, lemon juice, salt, and a few turns of pepper in a medium bowl and set aside for 5 to 10 minutes to soften the shallot. While whisking, slowly add the olive oil in a steady stream. The vinaigrette will keep, refrigerated in a covered container, for up to 1 week.

RAINBOW CARROT SALAD
with Millet, Feta, and Lemon Yogurt Dressing

Lemon Yogurt Dressing
(recipe follows)

1 bunch rainbow carrots,
with tops

¾ cup millet, cooked and
cooled to room temperature
(see page 40; about 3 cups
cooked millet)

¾ cup green or golden
raisins

½ cup hulled roasted and
salted sunflower seeds or
pepitas

1 cup whole fresh parsley
leaves

4 ounces feta cheese

Using all parts of the vegetable, like using all parts of the animal, is very trendy right now, and I respect any movement that rejects throwing away food. I use the tops from the carrots as the greens in this salad, but truth be told, carrot tops don't have a lot of flavor, so I tangle them together with parsley. This way I can feel good about the fact that I am not wasting the carrot tops, and also about the fact that my salad has flavor.

Being the native Californian that I am, I thought I knew raisins, but then I took a trip to my local Middle Eastern market and discovered a whole wall of raisin varieties, including two sizes of currants, jumbo raisins as big as dried cherries, and green raisins—not to be confused with golden raisins. Now that I've tasted green raisins, I'm like a slave to them. I still like black raisins in desserts because of their color, but for salads, green raisins own me. If you find them, try them. *Serves 4 to 6*

Reserve ¼ cup of the Lemon Yogurt Dressing and pour the rest into a bowl big enough to toss the entire salad.

Cut the tops off the carrots. Tear the carrot tops into small tufts. Rinse the carrot tops and put them on paper towels to dry. Shave the carrots into long ribbons using a U-shaped vegetable peeler.

Add the carrot ribbons to the bowl with the dressing and toss, making sure to coat the carrots with the dressing; your hands are the best tool for this, but a rubber spatula will also work. Add the millet, raisins, sunflower seeds, parsley, and carrot tops and give it all a gentle toss to combine. Crumble the feta over the salad and toss again gently. Drizzle the reserved dressing over the top.

recipe continues

TOSSING A SALAD

Your hands are the best tool for tossing salads. They allow you to massage the dressing onto the ingredients, so no bite is left undressed. You're also less likely to smash things up with your soft and malleable hands than you are with a big hard spoon or (heaven forbid!) salad tongs. Plus, a quote I've always attributed to James Beard but for the life of me cannot find online: hands are easy to clean, and you always know where they are.

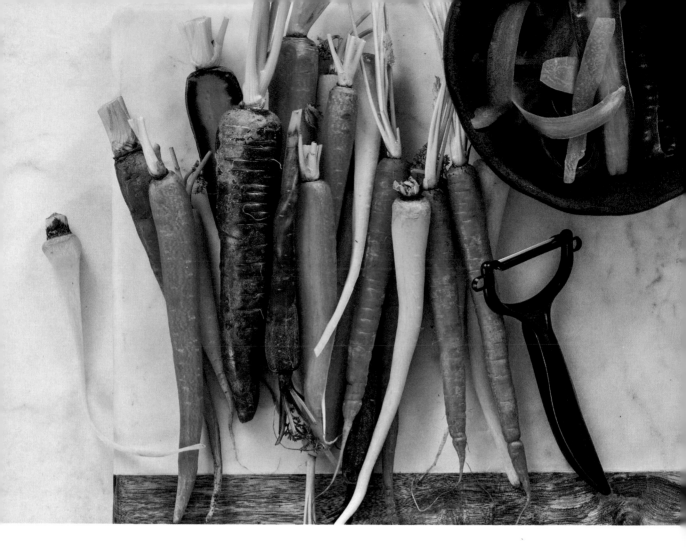

Lemon Yogurt Dressing

Makes about 1¼ cups

1 medium shallot, minced

⅓ cup fresh lemon juice (from about
1½ lemons)

2 tablespoons champagne vinegar or white
wine vinegar

2 teaspoons kosher salt

½ cup extra-virgin olive oil

¼ cup plus 2 tablespoons plain Greek
yogurt (or sheep's-milk yogurt)

Combine the shallot, lemon juice, vinegar,
and salt in a medium bowl and set aside
for 5 to 10 minutes to soften the shallot.
Add the olive oil in a steady stream,
whisking constantly. Put the yogurt in
a separate bowl and gradually add the
vinaigrette, whisking constantly. You add
the thin liquids to the yogurt gradually
to keep the dressing from breaking. The
yogurt vinaigrette will keep, refrigerated in
a covered container for up to 5 days.

ITALIAN ANTIPASTO RICE SALAD
with Tuna and Egg

1 cup long-grain brown rice, cooked and cooled to room temperature (see page 36; about 3½ cups cooked rice)

1 (6- to 8-ounce) jar olive oil–packed tuna

½ head radicchio, halved, cored, and shredded

1 (10- to 15-ounce) jar pepperoncini, stemmed and thinly sliced into rings

4 ounces thinly sliced salami, cut into ½-inch thick strips (optional)

Pepperoncini Vinaigrette (recipe follows)

1 cup fresh basil

1 cup fresh flat-leaf parsley

4 medium-boiled eggs (see page 59)

Kosher or sea salt and freshly ground black pepper

When my friend Silvia Baldini, a native of Turin, Italy, told me that a cold rice salad is a summertime staple in any Italian household, I knew I had to make it a staple in mine, too. Silvia is a chef living in Connecticut; she worked at Ottolenghi, the London restaurant behind the stunning book, *Plenty*, and she also competed and won on the reality cooking show *Chopped*, so I absolutely trust Silvia when it comes to all things cooking, especially Italian cooking. My rice salad is like an Italian antipasto platter reincarnated. Okay. So this may not be the healthiest salad in the book, but it is a healthy-ish way to enjoy an Italian antipasto salad, and that has to count for something. *Serves 4 to 6*

Put the rice in a big wide bowl. Crumble the tuna over the rice and add the radicchio, pepperoncini, and salami (if you're using it). Drizzle the vinaigrette over the salad and use scissors to snip the herbs over the bowl. Toss gently to combine the ingredients without breaking up the tuna any more than is inevitable. Lay the eggs on top of the salad and season them with salt and pepper.

Pepperoncini Vinaigrette

Makes about 2 cups

½ cup red wine vinegar

¼ cup pepperoncini pickling juice (from a jar of pepperoncini)

1 medium or large shallot, minced

2 teaspoons kosher salt

Freshly ground black pepper

1¼ cups extra-virgin olive oil

Combine the vinegar, pepperoncini pickling juice, shallot, salt, and several turns of pepper in a bowl and set aside for 5 to 10 minutes to soften the shallot. While whisking, slowly add the oil in a steady stream. The vinaigrette will keep, refrigerated, for up to 1 week.

RED BEET AND QUINOA SALAD
with Hazelnuts and Goat Cheese

FOR THE BEETS

1 bunch beets, trimmed and scrubbed

1 tablespoon olive oil

1 teaspoon kosher salt

Freshly ground black pepper

FOR THE SALAD

Balsamic Vinaigrette (recipe follows)

1 small to medium head radicchio, quartered, cored, and very thinly sliced, plus more whole leaves to use as cups (optional)

1 cup red, black, or tricolor quinoa, cooked and cooled to room temperature (see page 42; about 3½ cups cooked quinoa)

1 cup hazelnuts, toasted (see page 69) and coarsely chopped

3 ounces goat cheese (about 1 cup crumbled)

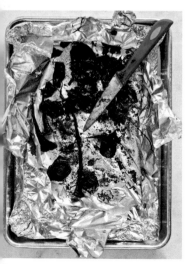

The one glorious year I had the good fortune to live in Venice Beach, California, I would walk into town on a fairly regular if not obsessive basis to pick up a quinoa and beet salad from GTA, the takeout store of the restaurant phenom Gjelina. When I moved from that neighborhood, I was forced to try to re-create the salad on my own, and this recipe is my re-creation.

Red beets stain anything they come into contact with. But in this salad, the red stain of the beet juice just makes the red quinoa and radicchio in this recipe *more red*, so the salad is fully committed to its redness. I sometimes use radicchio leaves as the "bowls" to serve the salad in, but if that's too cute for your taste, I totally understand.

In this method, the beets are wrapped in foil and then roasted in the oven, so it's really a combo of roasting and steaming, which gives you the deep, concentrated flavor effect of roasting beets while keeping the beets moist and juicy. *Serves 4 to 6*

To prepare the beets, adjust the oven racks so one is in the middle position and preheat the oven to 400°F.

Rip off a piece of heavy-duty aluminum foil (or doubled regular foil) big enough to enclose the beets. Put the beets on the foil and season with the olive oil, salt, and a few turns of pepper. Seal the beets in the foil and put the packet on a baking sheet. Roast the beets for about 1 hour 10 minutes, until they are tender when pierced with a toothpick or fork. Remove the beets from the oven and let the beets cool with the foil packets open. Peel the beets, wearing thin rubber gloves if you don't want to stain your fingers, and cut into ½-inch cubes.

Meanwhile, prepare the vinaigrette in a bowl large enough to toss the salad. Add the shredded radicchio and beets to the bowl with the vinaigrette and marinate for at least 10 minutes. Add the quinoa and hazelnuts, and stir to combine. Add the goat cheese in bite-size clumps and fold gently to distribute the cheese.

Balsamic Vinaigrette

Makes about 1¼ cups

1 medium or large shallot, minced

½ cup plus 2 tablespoons balsamic vinegar

Juice of 1 lemon

1 tablespoon kosher salt

⅔ cup extra-virgin olive oil

Combine the shallot, vinegar, lemon juice, and salt in a medium bowl and set aside for 5 to 10 minutes to soften the shallot. While whisking, slowly add the olive oil in a steady stream. The vinaigrette will keep, refrigerated in a covered container, for up to 1 week.

SHAVED BRUSSELS SPROUTS
with Spelt, Walnuts, and Pecorino

½ cup spelt, cooked and cooled to room temperature (see page 44; or farro or wheat berries; about 1 cup cooked grains)

1 pound Brussels sprouts

1½ cups walnuts, toasted (or hazelnuts or almonds; about 6 ounces), (see Toasting Nuts, page 69)

6 ounces Pecorino Romano, grated on the large holes of a box grater (about 1 heaping cup)

Sherry Vinaigrette (recipe follows)

Freshly ground black pepper

G-Free Alternative: To make this salad gluten-free, substitute sorghum, wild rice, or a combo of the two for the spelt in this recipe.

Shaved vegetable salads, and in particular shaved Brussels sprout salads, became part of our national food repertoire thanks, I believe, to my friend chef Jonathan Waxman. At his restaurant Barbuto, which, lucky for me, is conveniently located around the corner from my apartment in New York, Jonathan serves a shaved vegetable salad all year long, changing the vegetables with the season. I stole JW's idea and added hearty, chewy grains to make a meal of it. Substitute summer squash, shaved on a mandoline, asparagus, shaved lengthwise with a vegetable peeler, or carrots, shaved lengthwise with a vegetable peeler, for the Brussels sprouts in this recipe.

Shaving vegetables on a mandoline was a technique that freaked me out enough that I completely avoided it, until, testing a recipe for another cookbook, I was forced to confront my fear. In doing so, I discovered just how easy it actually is. *Serves 4 to 6*

Put the spelt in a big, wide bowl.

Holding a sprout at the stem end, press the top of the sprout against the mandoline to shave it, stopping just before you get uncomfortably close to your fingers. Discard the part you're holding and move on to the next sprout.

Add the shaved sprouts to the bowl with the spelt. Break the walnuts into pieces with your hands over the salad. Add the cheese, vinaigrette, and several turns of black pepper, and give the salad a good toss, ideally with your hands, to distribute the ingredients and coat them with the vinaigrette.

Sherry Vinaigrette

Makes about 1 cup

1 medium shallot, minced

¼ cup sherry vinegar

Juice of ½ lemon

2 teaspoons kosher salt

¼ cup plus 2 tablespoons extra-virgin olive oil

Combine the shallot, vinegar, lemon juice, and salt in a medium bowl and set aside for 5 to 10 minutes to soften the shallot. While whisking, add the olive oil in a slow stream and whisk until emulsified. The vinaigrette will keep, refrigerated in a covered container, for up to 1 week.

SESAME DUCK AND WILD RICE SALAD

FOR THE DUCK CONFIT

¼ cup kosher salt

1 tablespoon light or dark brown sugar

Freshly ground black pepper

4 duck legs

4 cups duck fat

Olive oil (or canola oil), as needed

FOR THE SALAD

½ cup wild rice, cooked and cooled to room temperature (see page 45; about 3 cups cooked rice)

½ head napa cabbage, cored and thinly sliced (about 4 cups)

4 scallions, white and light green parts only, thinly sliced on an angle

¼ cup toasted white sesame seeds, plus more for garnish

2 Fresno or serrano chiles, stemmed and thinly sliced into rings

Sesame Dressing (recipe follows)

This duck salad is inspired by Asian noodle salad, with wild rice in place of the noodles. The duck in this recipe is duck *confit*, which is duck cooked in duck fat. Like so many foods we know and love (bacon, anyone?), this technique originated as a way of preserving duck, but we now use it as a means of making *delicious* duck. You can buy duck fat just about everywhere that duck is sold; I buy it at my local butcher shop. If you don't want to or don't have the hours it takes to make the duck, you can also buy duck confit already prepared and sealed in cryovac: the French idea of fast food. *Serves 4*

To prepare the duck, combine the salt, sugar, and several turns of black pepper in a bowl. One at a time, put the duck legs in the bowl with the seasonings and sprinkle and pat the rub to coat the legs all over. Put the duck legs in a zip-top bag or in a glass or ceramic baking dish. Close the bag or cover the dish with plastic wrap. Refrigerate the duck overnight or for at least 4 hours.

Adjust the oven racks so one is in the middle position and preheat the oven to 325°F.

Heat the duck fat in a medium saucepan over medium heat to liquify it. Remove the duck from the refrigerator and rinse off the rub. Pat the legs dry with paper towels and put them in a baking dish just big enough to hold them in a single layer. Pour the duck fat over them; if you don't have enough duck fat to cover the legs, add oil to cover. Cover the dish with foil and bake the duck until it is fork tender (you'll be able to twist a fork easily when you pierce it into the meat), about 1½ hours. Remove the duck from the oven, uncover, and leave it in the fat to cool completely. Remove the duck from the fat. Strain the fat and refrigerate it until you are ready to use it again.

To prepare the salad, shred the duck meat into a big bowl; discard the skin and bones. Add the wild rice, cabbage, scallions, sesame seeds, and sliced chiles. Drizzle with half the dressing and toss, making sure to coat the cabbage thoroughly with the dressing (I like to do this with my hands). Add more dressing as desired. Sprinkle with sesame seeds, and serve.

Sesame Dressing

Makes about 1 cup

¼ cup low-sodium soy sauce or tamari

¼ cup mirin (Japanese sweet rice wine; substitute dry sherry)

¼ cup raw or granulated sugar

¼ cup tahini

½ teaspoon kosher salt

Put all the ingredients in a clean jam or mustard jar with a lid and give the jar a good shake to combine and to dissolve the sugar. (You could also do this in a bowl with a whisk.) The dressing will keep, refrigerated, for up to several weeks.

UMBRIAN FARRO AND BEAN SALAD
with Celery Leaf Pesto and Mozzarella

¾ cup farro, cooked and cooled to room temperature (see page 37; about 2 cups cooked farro)

1½ cups Italian-Style Beans (page 104) or 1 (15-ounce) canned borlotti beans, chickpeas, or white beans, drained

Celery Leaf Pesto (recipe follows)

4 to 6 celery stalks, thinly sliced into half-moons (the innermost, lightest green stalks of celery are the most tender and tastiest)

2 tablespoons champagne vinegar or white wine vinegar

2 tablespoons extra-virgin olive oil

1 teaspoon kosher salt

8 ounces bocconcini (or another fresh mozzarella cut into bite-size pieces)

G-Free Alternative: To make this g-free, try it with sorghum or wild rice.

Lemon juice causes pesto and other herb sauces to turn an unappealing, dull shade of green. Adding it just before serving means a brighter, prettier pesto. What can I say? When it comes to food, looks matter.

I came up with the idea of tossing beans in celery leaf pesto one summer, when I was co-hosting a party in Umbria with Nancy Silverton for the filming of the PBS show *I'll Have What Phil's Having*. I began to look through cookbooks at Nancy's house, where I was staying, to get ideas. Nancy wanted everything to be served at room temperature, so that all the cooking could be done early and there would be nothing to do when the guests and film crew arrived except ask, "Red or white?" My method for finding inspiration was to sit on the front porch overlooking the medieval town and the olive groves below, and flip through a huge stack of cookbooks to see what stuck in my head the next day. Only one thing did, and that was a version of this salad with beans tossed in celery leaf pesto. I went a little crazy and added mozzarella and farro. *Serves 4*

Put farro and beans in a large bowl. Add three-fourths of the pesto, the celery, vinegar, oil, and salt and toss gently to mix all the ingredients together and coat the farro and beans with the pesto. Add more pesto if desired. Add the mozzarella and toss gently to combine the ingredients, being careful not to smash the mozzarella.

Celery Leaf Pesto

This pesto is made with the leaves from one bunch of celery, and parsley. If you're short celery leaves, make up for it in parsley. *Makes about 2 cups*

1 cup packed fresh celery leaves (all the leaves from 1 bunch; discard the really tough dark green outer leaves)

1 cup packed fresh flat-leaf parsley

½ cup extra-virgin olive oil, plus more as needed

¼ cup finely grated Parmesan cheese

1 tablespoon pine nuts, toasted (see page 69)

2 garlic cloves

1 teaspoon kosher salt

Juice of 1 lemon

Put all the ingredients except the lemon juice in a blender or food processor and blend until the pesto is smooth with some flecks, stopping once or twice to scrape down the side of the blender. The pesto should be loose and spoonable, not globby; if it's too thick, add more oil and blend it in. Stir in the lemon juice just before serving. Refrigerate leftover pesto in a covered container for up to 2 days; it will lose its pretty color with time but it will still taste great. Bring it to room temperature before using.

ITALIAN-STYLE BEANS

I contemplated whether or not to give a recipe for cooking dried beans because using canned is so easy. I decided to include it because cooking dried beans is pretty darned easy, too—and homemade beans are infinitely more delicious than canned. (Hummus (page 185) made from homemade chickpeas? Forget it!) Making beans yourself will also cost you a lot less, bean for bean. Pretty much everything on this ingredient list is optional—just use what you have. The beans will last, refrigerated, for up to 5 days. You can also freeze the beans in their cooking liquid.

Makes about 2 quarts

---

1 pound dried chickpeas, cannellini (white) beans, or borlotti (cranberry) beans, soaked overnight and drained

2 tablespoons extra-virgin olive oil

2 tablespoons kosher salt

1 Spanish yellow onion, peeled and halved

1 head garlic, halved crosswise

1 carrot, halved (optional; use it if you have it)

1 celery stalk, halved (optional; use it if you have it)

1 long rosemary sprig (optional; use it if you have it)

1 bay leaf (optional; use it if you have it)

1 árbol chile pod (optional; use it if you have it)

Put the beans in a large pot. Add the olive oil, salt, onion, garlic, and whatever optional ingredients you are using. Add enough water to cover the beans by 2 or 3 inches. Bring the water to a boil over high heat, reduce the heat to maintain a simmer, and cook gently until the beans are tender and not the least bit chalky in the middle, about 1. hours, adding more water as necessary to keep them covered by an inch or two. Turn off the heat. Remove the garlic, squeeze the cloves out of the head into the beans, and discard the garlic skins. You can remove the other vegetables or just serve around them; I do the latter.

SORGHUM GREEK SALAD

½ cup sorghum, cooked and cooled to room temperature (see Sorghum, page 43; about 1 cup cooked grains)

3 Persian cucumbers (or 1 hothouse or English cucumber)

1 bunch radishes

White Balsamic Vinaigrette (recipe follows)

½ small or medium red onion, thinly sliced into half moons

1 pint small sweet tomatoes, halved and lightly salted

4 ounces feta (about 1 cup crumbled)

1 cup fresh Italian parsley, basil, and oregano or marjoram (combine them in whatever amounts you like or have to get to 1 cup)

I never get tired of the combination of flavors in a Greek salad; adding grains to the salad makes it feel like a real meal. It also turns it into a hit, bring-a-salad salad for any summertime gathering. Sorghum has a neutral flavor, so this is almost like a pasta salad. It's also g-free. If gluten isn't an issue, consider substituting wheat berries or farro for the sorghum; those grains have an earthier flavor, and they are also grains you'd find in Greece, if you're looking for authenticity. *Serves 4 to 6*

Put the sorghum in a large, wide bowl.

Slice the cucumbers into ¼-inch-thin rounds and toss them into the bowl with the sorghum. Scrub the radishes and trim and discard the greens, leaving a bit of the stems attached to use as a handle. Holding the radishes by the stem, thinly slice them as on a mandoline, or slice them as thin as humanly possible with a knife. Add the radishes to the bowl with the cucumbers and sorghum and add the onions and tomatoes.

Drizzle the vinaigrette over the salad and give it a gentle toss with a big spoon or rubber spatula. Crumble the feta over the salad. Grab the herbs, clump them up as tightly as possible, and use scissors to cut them over the bowl so they fall into the salad. Toss gently to combine the ingredients without smashing the cheese.

White Balsamic Vinaigrette
Makes about 1 cup

1 medium shallot, minced

½ cup white balsamic vinegar (or white wine vinegar plus 1 teaspoon honey)

Juice of ½ lemon

1 teaspoon salt

½ cup extra-virgin olive oil

Combine the shallot, vinegar, lemon juice, and salt in a medium bowl and set aside for 5 to 10 minutes to soften the shallot. While whisking, slowly add the olive oil in a steady stream. The vinaigrette will keep, refrigerated in a covered container, for up to 1 week.

WINTER WILD RICE SALAD
with Dates and Parmesan

1 cup wild rice, cooked and cooled to room temperature (see page 45; about 3 cups cooked wild rice)

5 celery stalks, plus the leaves from the whole bunch of celery

1 fennel bulb

1 cup whole almonds, toasted (see page 69) and coarsely chopped

15 to 20 large dates, pitted and thinly sliced lengthwise

4 to 5 ounces Parmesan cheese, shaved or very thinly sliced

Strips of zest of 1 orange (zested with a channel zester)

Orange Vinaigrette (recipe follows)

My mom lives in the Palm Springs area, so whenever she comes to visit, I ask her to bring dates from a date farm not far from her house. Not that they don't have dates for sale in San Diego and New York, where I live, but there's something special about someone bringing foods straight from where it was grown or made, don't you think? Dates are a dried fruit, but some are fresher than others. Look for sticky, gooey dates, which you can find at farmers' markets if you live in Southern California, or in the produce section of the supermarket. This salad makes a delicious take-to-wherever lunch or side dish for Thanksgiving, or any meal with a fall feeling. This salad is vegetarian and gluten-free. To make it vegan, lose the Parm. *Serves 4 to 6*

Put the wild rice in a large bowl.

Thinly slice the celery stalks and throw the slices into the bowl with the rice. Add the celery leaves. Quarter the fennel bulb, cut out and discard the cores, and thinly slice each quarter lengthwise to create matchsticks; throw the matchsticks into the bowl. Add the almonds, dates, Parmesan, and orange zest. Drizzle the vinaigrette over the salad and toss.

Orange Vinaigrette

Makes about 1 cup

1 medium shallot, minced

¼ cup fresh orange juice

2 tablespoons champagne vinegar or white wine vinegar

2 teaspoons kosher salt

Freshly ground black pepper

¼ cup plus 2 tablespoons extra-virgin olive oil

Combine the shallot, orange juice, vinegar, salt, and several turns of pepper in a medium bowl and set aside for 5 to 10 minutes to soften the shallot. While whisking, slowly add the oil in a steady stream. The vinaigrette will keep, refrigerated in a covered container, for up to a week.

CHINESE CHICKEN SALAD
with Toasted Almonds and Crispy Rice

FOR THE CHICKEN

2 egg whites

¼ cup cornstarch

¼ teaspoon white pepper
(or black pepper)

½ teaspoon kosher salt

2 skinless boneless chicken
breasts

Canola oil (or another
neutral-flavored oil)

FOR THE SALAD

1 cup long- or short-grain
brown rice, cooked (see
page 36; about 3½ cups
cooked rice) and cooled to
room temperature

1 tablespoon canola oil
(or another neutral-flavored
oil)

1 teaspoon kosher salt

1½ cups slivered almonds,
toasted (see page 69)

3 clementines (or seedless
tangerines), peeled and
segmented

1 bunch scallions, thinly
sliced into rounds

1 head napa cabbage (or
iceberg lettuce), cored and
thinly sliced

Ginger Vinaigrette (recipe
follows)

My guilty pleasure when I lived in Los Angeles was the Chinese chicken salad at Joan's on Third, a very popular, beautifully styled prepared food store in the center of West Hollywood. It went like this: If I were anywhere near Joan's and I'd had a hard day or if I felt lonely or I was busy packing for a trip or if I simply felt, for whatever reason, like I deserved a treat, I turned my mind to that Chinese chicken salad and said to myself: *You deserve this.* Even though it has the word "salad" in its name, I wasn't to be fooled. There was nothing nutritionally beneficial about this salad; it was mostly iceberg lettuce and crunchy deep-fried wonton strips, all drenched in a sweet gingery dressing. I make this salad with Joan's salad in mind, but I use cabbage instead of iceberg and toss it with crispy brown rice in place of the fried wontons in a nod to healthy. The chicken is "velveted," which means it's dredged in cornstarch before being pan-fried, giving it a silky exterior that's like halfway to fried chicken. *Serves 4 to 6*

To prepare the chicken, whisk the egg whites, cornstarch, pepper, and salt together in a medium bowl. One at a time, pound the chicken breasts between two sheets of waxed or parchment paper with a meat mallet or the back of a small, heavy skillet until they are an even ½ inch thick. Dredge the chicken breasts in the bowl with the cornstarch mixture and turn to coat them. Cover and refrigerate for at least 20 minutes and up to several hours.

Remove the chicken from the refrigerator. Pour enough oil in a large skillet to coat it and heat the oil over medium-high heat until it slides like water in the pan and is sizzling hot but not smoking, 2 to 3 minutes. Lift the chicken breasts out of the cornstarch mixture, letting the excess drip back into the bowl.

Lay the chicken in the pan and cook until it is golden brown on one side, 3 to 4 minutes. Resist the temptation to fiddle with the chicken; it will brown better if you leave it alone. Flip the chicken breasts, reduce the heat to medium, and cook the breasts on the second side for about 3 minutes, until cooked through. (To test for doneness, pierce it with a small sharp knife; if the juices run clear, it's done. If the juices are pink, it needs to cook longer.) Put the chicken breasts on a plate or cutting board and let them rest before slicing. Slice into ½-inch-thick pieces.

To make the salad, arrange the oven racks so one is in the middle position and preheat the oven to 300°F.

recipe continues

Dump the rice onto a baking sheet, drizzle with the oil, sprinkle with the salt, and toss to distribute. Bake the rice until it's crispy, about 30 minutes, stirring it with a spatula once or twice while it cooks so it crisps evenly and doesn't burn. Remove the rice from the oven and dump it out into a large, wide bowl to cool to room temperature.

Add the chicken slices, almonds, clementine segments, scallions, and cabbage to the bowl with the cooled rice. Drizzle with the Ginger Vinaigrette and toss up the whole story, ideally with your hands so you can massage the vinaigrette onto the cabbage without smashing it.

Ginger Vinaigrette

Makes about 1¼ cups

½ cup rice vinegar

2 tablespoons sugar

1 teaspoon ground white pepper (or black pepper)

1 (3-inch) piece fresh ginger, peeled and grated on a Microplane or minced (about 1 tablespoon)

1½ teaspoons kosher salt

½ cup canola oil (or another neutral-flavored oil)

Combine the vinegar, sugar, pepper, ginger, and salt in a medium bowl and whisk to combine. While whisking, slowly add the oil in a steady stream. The vinaigrette will keep, refrigerated in a covered container, for up to 1 week.

BROCCOLINI AND SPROUT SALAD
with Poppy Seed Dressing and Avocado

1 cup unhulled barley, cooked and cooled to room temperature (see page 34; about 2 cups cooked barley)

6 ounces (about 2 cups) mixed crunchy sprouts (from sprouted beans such as mung beans, chickpeas, lentils, or peas)

1 bunch Broccolini

½ cup hulled roasted salted sunflower seeds

1 teaspoon poppy seeds, plus more for garnish

Poppy Seed Dressing (recipe follows)

½ cup broccoli sprouts (or clover sprouts or alfalfa sprouts)

2 avocados, halved, pitted, peeled, and cut into ½-inch cubes

Kosher salt

G-Free Alternative: To make this gluten-free, use wild rice or sorghum.

I was raised in Southern California in the 1970s, so I've eaten my share of poppy seed dressing, globbed out straight from the bottle onto piles of iceberg lettuce or into a pitted avocado. For decades, I turned my back on that cloying, viscous dressing. But then, at some point in life, you embrace your history. You realize you are going to die (someday) and that it's okay to love what you grew up to love. And, if you're me, you learn to make poppy seed dressing.

I may be prouder of this salad than of any other recipe in this book because I took a childhood memory and turned it into something modern and healthy and so darned tasty I want to tell the world. I call for barley because I think of it as an old-school grain, something we were eating during the salad days of poppy seed dressing, long before quinoa steamrolled into our lives. *Serves 4 to 6*

Combine the barley and crunchy sprouts in a big bowl. Cut off and discard the tough ends of the Broccolini. Snap or cut the florets off the stems and cut or break them into small florets to mirror the size of the sprouted beans and grains. Throw them into the bowl with the grains and sprouts. Trim and discard the tough ends from the stems. Thinly slice the remaining stems crosswise and throw them into the bowl. Add the sunflower seeds and poppy seeds.

Drizzle the dressing over the salad and toss with a rubber spatula or your hands, making sure to coat all the veggie bits with the dressing. Pull the broccoli sprouts apart into small clumps and drop them into the salad. Sprinkle the avocado cubes with salt and add them to the salad. Toss gently to disperse the sprouts and avocado throughout the salad without smashing them. Sprinkle with poppy seeds, and serve.

recipe continues

Poppy Seed Dressing

Makes about 1¼ cups

1 egg yolk

2 teaspoons Dijon mustard

¾ cup canola oil (or another neutral-flavored oil)

2 tablespoons champagne vinegar or white wine vinegar

2 tablespoons grated Spanish yellow onion (from about ¼ medium onion, grated on a microplane)

2 tablespoons honey

Juice of ½ lemon

2 teaspoons poppy seeds

1½ teaspoons kosher salt

Combine the egg yolk and mustard in a medium bowl that will be easy to whisk in, such as a slope-sided glass or stainless-steel bowl. Start whisking, then add the oil to the bowl drop by drop, whisking constantly, until an emulsion forms (see Making an Emulsion, page 114). Still whisking, begin to drizzle in the oil in a slow steady stream; as the emulsion begins to get very thick, add a splash of the vinegar to thin it. Do this a few times as you are adding the oil until you've added all the vinegar and all of the oil. Add the onion, honey, lemon juice, poppy seeds, and salt and stir to combine. The dressing will keep, refrigerated in a covered container, for up to 1 week.

MAKING AN EMULSION

When a sauce or dressing emulsifies, it means the distinct liquids are suspended amid one another rather than segregating themselves in the same container. Once emulsified, the molecules live in their new formation; they don't separate into, say, oil and water after you quit whisking. It's like marriage without divorce. You can recognize an emulsified dressing as one that is thick and creamy. Mayonnaise, for example, is an emulsification of egg and oil, and once the egg and oil are emulsified, they're mayonnaise forever. Some salad dressings are emulsified; you whisk them together until they are one, and then, no matter what, they *stay* one. Caesar salad dressing, made correctly, is an emulsified dressing, and so is poppy seed dressing. Non-emulsified dressings, including many vinaigrettes, come together when you whisk them, but then separate the moment you turn your back. You know the type.

Making an emulsion isn't difficult, but it does take patience. The secret is to add the thinner liquid to the thicker one (the oil to the egg, for example) in excruciatingly slow increments, whisking all the while. Drop. By. Yes. Only. One. Keep. Whisking. Okay. Now. Add. Another. Drop. By adding the oil in this way, you are able to suspend the oil molecules amid the egg molecules. You'll know you've formed an emulsion when the mixture becomes thick and creamy and opaque. At this point you can drizzle instead of drop the oil in. I wouldn't say "quickly," but you won't have time to lose your mind between droplets, either.

Just when you thought you had the hang of it, there's this: When you're making an emulsion, if it gets *too* thick, it will separate. It just can't stand the weight of itself. The cure for this is to add a few droplets of water (or whatever thin liquids you are adding to the emulsion). In the case of Caesar dressing, those thin liquids are lime juice, Tabasco, and Worcestershire sauce. In the case of poppy seed dressing or mayonnaise, it would be lemon, vinegar, and maybe also water.

When you're making an emulsified dressing or mayonnaise, the bowl will rock around a lot as a result of your vigorous whisking. You have a few options for keeping it in place: you can wrap a wet dishtowel around the base of the bowl; drape a dishtowel over a small saucepan and set the bowl on top of the saucepan; or have someone stand next to you and hold it.

If, despite all your efforts, your emulsion breaks, you'll know it because instead of looking creamy and opaque, the mixture will look like two distinct ingredients floating independently. The best way to fix it is to put a fresh egg yolk in a bowl and treat the stuff in the first bowl, the broken emulsion, as if it were the oil, adding it, just as you should have done with the oil the first time around: Drop. By. Painstakingly. Slow. Drop. If you want, you can double the rest of the ingredients in the recipe to make up for the extra egg yolk. Or not. A little extra egg yolk never killed anyone.

MAIN BOWLS

This chapter is large because it contains all main-dish bowls, and the reason is simple. Dividing it up in the typical cookbook style—vegetarian, seafood, poultry, etc.—didn't work in bowl world, because bowls are so flexible. With few exceptions, any one of these main bowls can contain any protein, any vegetarian bowl can have meat added, and the meat can be eliminated from any meat-centric bowl. Throughout this chapter, in addition to the composed bowls, you'll see big photo spreads along with a list of components for building your own Asian, Mexican, Middle Eastern, and Farmers' Market–Inspired bowls. Use these as jumping-off points for combining ingredients to create your own bowls, or for entertaining. Grain bowls are meant to be healthy and delicious, whimsical and comforting. Make them whatever you want them to be.

SAMBAL TOFU QUINOA BOWL with Sesame Spring Veggies 119

VIETNAMESE BOWL with Sweet and Tangy Vinaigrette 120

FARMERS' MARKET BOWL with Yogurt Green Goddess and Salty Pepitas 123

SPICY TUNA TARTARE with Brown Sushi Rice and Avocado 126

MILLET POLENTA with Wild Mushrooms and Parmesan 129

SALMON POKE BOWL with Brown Rice and Edamame 130

WARM CHICKEN CAESAR BOWL with Quinoa and Kale 131

GLAZED PORK BELLY with Ginger Scallion Rice and Pickled Vegetables 133

BUILD YOUR OWN ASIAN BOWL 136

CHICKEN OR TOFU SATAY BOWL with Coconut Rice 138

SPICED RICE AND LENTILS with Seared Halloumi 141

SUMMER CORN FARROTTO with Brown Butter and Sweet Burst Tomatoes 144

BURNT VEGETABLE BOWL with Black Rice and Lentils and Tahini Sauce 147

BUTTERNUT SQUASH RISOTTO with Slow-Cooked Kale 149

GRAVEYARD RICE with Bone Marrow and Parsley Salad 151

BUILD YOUR OWN FARMERS' MARKET-INSPIRED BOWL 153

CHINO RANCH VEGETABLE BOWL with Kale Pistachio Pesto and Bagna Cauda 154

MOROCCAN MILLET with Braised Root Vegetables and Harissa 157

FIVE-SPICE RIBLETS with Sticky Rice and Apple Slaw 160

COCONUT CURRY RICE BOWL with Green Vegetables and Sweet Potatoes 164

POMEGRANATE TABBOULEH with Crunchy Falafel, Baba-G, and Tahini Sauce 167

BUILD YOUR OWN MIDDLE EASTERN BOWL 172

MOLE TEFF AND CHICKEN with Avocado and Crema 174

CHILE EN NOGADA BOWL with Turkey Picadillo and Walnut Crema 178

RED RICE PAD THAI with Tofu and Shrimp 182

MEZZE BOWL with Pomegranate-Glazed Lamb Meatballs, Hummus, and Tzatziki 183

SUNDAY NIGHT DETOX BOWL with Roasted Broccoli and Ponzu 186

BUILD YOUR OWN MEXICAN BOWL 191

ULTIMATE BURRITO BOWL 192

KOREAN SHORT RIBS with Kimchi Rice 196

BAJA BBQ SHRIMP BOWL with Corn Rice 199

INDIAN CAULIFLOWER AND CHICKPEA CURRY with Savory Yogurt and Millet 202

SORGHUM RISOTTO PRIMAVERA with Bacon and Burrata 205

BRAZILIAN BOWL with Quick-Cooked Collards and Ají 206

SAMBAL TOFU QUINOA BOWL
with Sesame Spring Veggies

FOR THE TOFU

¼ cup low-sodium soy sauce or tamari

3 tablespoons sambal oelek (or another Asian chile garlic paste)

1 tablespoon honey (or maple syrup or agave syrup)

1 (12- to 16-ounce) package firm tofu, drained and cut into 1-inch cubes

Canola oil (or another neutral-flavored oil)

FOR THE VEGETABLES

Canola oil (or another neutral-flavored oil)

1 bunch asparagus (preferably thick spears), cut into 2-inch segments

1 cup sugar snap peas, strings removed

2 teaspoons kosher salt

1 teaspoon toasted sesame oil (optional; use it if you have it)

2 tablespoons toasted sesame seeds (white or black or a mix)

Maldon, fleur de sel, or another flaky sea salt

1 head green cabbage, cut into 6 wedges

FOR THE BOWL

1 cup quinoa, cooked (or Ginger Scallion Rice, long-grain brown rice, or black rice, see pages 42, 135, 36, and 35; about 3½ cups cooked grains)

4 scallions, white and light green parts only, thinly sliced on an angle

I'm a card-carrying, fat-loving, flavor-hoarding omnivore—plus, I once read that tofu, being as processed as it is, is "the white flour of the health food world." All this to say that if I'm going to eat tofu, I'm going to eat it for one reason: because it tastes great. These tofu cubes, light and custardy on the inside and doused in sweet chile paste on the outside, fit that bill. They couldn't be better if they were pork. And the vegetables couldn't be easier. Get a pan sizzling hot, throw in the vegetables, give them a toss. The one thing to keep in mind is not to overcrowd the pan. Each and every piece has contact with the hot surface. The color you get on them from that direct heat is what gives them the flavor we all love. Otherwise, we'd all still be talking about how much we love boiled and steamed vegetables, which we're not. Use this recipe to prepare green beans, red and yellow bell peppers, eggplant, and zucchini in the summer; or Broccolini, broccoli, kale, cabbage, and carrots, which are available and flavorful year-round. I like to use thick asparagus spears; thinner spears are too easy to overcook. *Serves 4*

To prepare the tofu, stir the soy sauce, chile paste, and honey together in a large bowl. Add the tofu cubes and set aside to marinate while you prepare the rest of the components, or for at least 20 minutes. Remove the tofu cubes from the marinade with a slotted spoon, reserving the marinade, and put them on paper towels to dry. Set the bowl with the marinade aside.

Pour enough canola oil into a large skillet to coat it and heat it over medium-high heat until the oil slides like water in the pan and is searing hot but not smoking, 2 to 3 minutes. Add the tofu cubes and fry until they are golden brown, turning with tongs to brown all sides, 6 to 8 minutes. Remove the tofu from the pan and place it in the bowl with the marinade. Give the tofu a quick toss with a rubber spatula or spoon to coat the cubes.

To prepare the vegetables, pour enough canola oil into a large skillet to coat it and heat over medium-high heat until the oil

slides like water in the pan and is searing hot but not smoking, 2 to 3 minutes. Add the asparagus and sugar snaps, sprinkle with 1 teaspoon of the salt, and sear them, tossing the pan or otherwise turning the veggies, for about 1 minute, until they are beginning to blister on the outside but are still crunchy. Slide the veggies out of the pan into a big bowl and toss with the sesame oil (if you are using it), sesame seeds, and a pinch of sea salt.

Add a bit more oil to the pan, heat it until it slides like water in the pan and is almost smoking, and add the cabbage wedges. Sprinkle the cabbage with the remaining 1 teaspoon salt and cook until the wedges are seared on all three sides, turning them with tongs as they brown, about 3 minutes per side.

To serve, spoon the quinoa into four bowls and tumble the tofu cubes and sauce on top. Serve the veggies to the side of the tofu and drop the scallions over the whole picture.

VIETNAMESE BOWL
with Sweet and Tangy Vinaigrette

FOR THE PROTEIN

¼ cup rice vinegar

¼ cup sesame oil

2 tablespoons low-sodium soy sauce or tamari

2 tablespoons honey

4 (4-ounce) skinless salmon fillets; 1 pound large shrimp, peeled and deveined; 2 skinless boneless chicken breasts; or 1 package firm tofu, drained and cut into 1-inch slabs

Kosher salt

Canola oil (or another neutral-flavored oil)

FOR THE BOWLS

1 cup brown rice or quinoa, cooked (see page 36 or 42; about 3½ cups cooked grains)

½ head purple, green, or napa cabbage, cored and very thinly sliced

2 cups bean sprouts

2 large carrots, shaved into long ribbons with a U-shaped vegetable peeler

4 scallions (white and light green parts only)

1 cup fresh cilantro, mint, and/or basil (preferably Thai basil)

2 red Fresno chiles (or red or green serrano or jalapeño chiles), stemmed and very thinly sliced

Sweet and Tangy Vinaigrette (recipe follows)

1 cup roasted salted peanuts (or cashews), coarsely chopped

If I were to nominate one place as ground zero for the bowl movement, I'd name Axe (pronounced *ah-shay*), a (sadly) now closed restaurant in Los Angeles that was serving delicious healthy food long before "eating clean" became part of our culinary lexicon. The Axe bowl is what happens when a Vietnamese rice bowl meets the Santa Monica Farmers Market: a scoop of steamed quinoa or brown rice in an enormous bowl topped with salmon, shrimp, chicken, or tofu, crunchy veggies and herbs, and a sweet, tangy vinaigrette. For me, ordering a "bowl" at Axe was not even a matter of free will because if I ordered anything else, I'd find myself looking around the room with bowl envy. RIP, Axe.

This bowl is naturally g-free and, like at Axe, you choose your protein: salmon, shrimp, chicken, or tofu. They all use the same marinade so you could even offer a selection; just remember not to marinate chicken with anything else because of the dangers of salmonella. *Serves 4*

To prepare the protein, combine the vinegar, sesame oil, soy sauce, and honey in a glass or ceramic baking dish or bowl, or in a large zip-top bag. Put the fish, shrimp, chicken, or tofu in the marinade, turn to coat, and cover the bowl or close the bag. Refrigerate for 30 to 45 minutes for fish or shrimp, up to 2 hours for chicken or tofu. Remove the protein from the marinade and season with salt.

Pour enough canola oil into a large sauté pan to coat it lightly and heat it over medium-high heat until the oil slides easily in the pan and is sizzling hot but not smoking, 2 to 3 minutes; the protein should sizzle when it hits the pan.

For salmon, put the fish in the pan, rounded-side down, and cook until golden brown and caramelized, about 4 minutes. Carefully turn the salmon, reduce the heat to medium-low, and cook for about 4 minutes, until it looks medium-rare from the side. Remove the salmon from the pan.

For shrimp, cook until they are pink and opaque on both sides, about 5 minutes total.

For chicken, lay the chicken breasts in the skillet and cook until the first side is caramelized, about 3 minutes. Turn, reduce the heat to medium, and cook for about 5 minutes, until the chicken is cooked through. (The juices will run clear when

recipe continues

the chicken is pierced with a small sharp knife, and the chicken will register 165°F on an instant-read thermometer.) Remove the chicken from the skillet and let it rest for 5 minutes before slicing it.

For tofu, cook until it is seared on each side, about 3 minutes per side. Remove it from the skillet and thinly slice it.

Spoon the rice into four bowls. Put one portion of protein on each bowl.

Drop a handful each of the cabbage, bean sprouts, carrots, and scallions around the protein and scatter the herbs and chiles over the top. Drizzle 2 tablespoons of the vinaigrette over the vegetables and rain on the nuts. Serve the remaining vinaigrette and any remaining vegetables in little bowls on the side.

Sweet and Tangy Vinaigrette

Makes about 1¼ cups

½ cup canola oil (or another neutral-flavored oil)

½ cup rice vinegar

1 (3- to 4-inch) piece fresh ginger, peeled and grated on a Microplane or minced (about 1 heaping tablespoon)

3 tablespoons fresh lime juice (from about 2 limes)

1 generous tablespoon honey

2 garlic cloves, grated on a Microplane or minced

1 teaspoon kosher salt

Combine all the ingredients in a clean jam or mustard jar with a lid and give the jar a good shake. (You could also do this in a bowl with a whisk.) The vinaigrette will keep, refrigerated, for up to a week.

FARMERS' MARKET BOWL
with Yogurt Green Goddess and Salty Pepitas

FOR THE ROASTED VEGETABLES

1 acorn squash, halved lengthwise, seeded, and sliced into ½-inch half-moons

½ pound Brussels sprouts, trimmed and halved

1 bunch carrots with greens, scrubbed and halved lengthwise (leaving 1 inch of greens attached)

3 tablespoons olive oil

2½ teaspoons kosher salt

Freshly ground black pepper

FOR THE BOWLS

Yogurt Green Goddess (recipe follows)

1 cup Khorasan wheat, cooked (or farro or spelt, see page 39, 37, or 44)

1 head radicchio, sliced

1½ cups cooked chickpeas (see page 104), or 1 (15-ounce) can, drained and rinsed

2 medium-cooked eggs (see page 59), cut in half

Kosher salt

Freshly ground black pepper

1 cup roasted salted pepitas (pumpkin seeds)

1 cup radish sprouts (or another type of sprouts or microgreens), optional

G-Free Alternative: To make this gluten-free, substitute wild rice, quinoa, or sorghum, or a combination, for the Khorasan wheat.

The beauty of the squash and carrots in this bowl is the color you achieve when they're roasted. The color is the result of what is referred to as caramelization. That the root of this word is *caramel* is no coincidence. Roasting vegetables brings out their natural sweetness. Winter squash keeps at room temperature for weeks, if not months. During the fall and winter, I keep a display of assorted squash in my house, so I can admire their beauty while also having them to cook for hunger emergencies. You can roast cauliflower, fennel, or sliced sweet potatoes—in place of the vegetables called for here.

This recipe is vegetarian. To make it vegan, skip the egg and dress the bowl with Tahini Sauce (page 148) in place of the Yogurt Green Goddess. *Serves 4*

To cook the vegetables, arrange the oven racks so one is in the middle and none is near the oven floor; you are going to put the baking sheet on the oven floor. (If you have an oven that doesn't allow you to put a baking sheet on the floor, put the rack as close to the floor as possible.) Preheat the oven to 500°F.

Toss the vegetables in a big bowl with the oil, salt, and pepper and lay them flat on two baking sheets, making sure not to overcrowd them. (If you overcrowd the baking sheets, the vegetables will steam instead of caramelizing.) Put one baking sheet on the middle rack and one on the floor of the oven or the lowest rack and roast for 10 to 12 minutes, rotating the baking sheets and turning the veggies midway through the baking time so they brown evenly. (I turn the vegetables one by one with tongs to get perfect browning, but if you'd rather just give them a good shake, I hear you.) Remove the vegetables from the oven.

To prepare the bowls, smear a big spoonful of the green goddess in the bottom of each bowl. Scoop the grains into the bowl, and arrange the radicchio, roasted vegetables, and chickpeas on top. Nestle an egg half in the center of each. Season the eggs with salt and pepper, and scatter the pepitas and sprouts, if using, over the bowls. Serve with more green goddess on the side to drizzle at will.

recipe continues

NOTE ON THE OVEN FLOOR

Putting a sheet pan directly on the oven floor is a trick I learned from a chef friend who had gone from working in restaurants with super powerful ovens to cooking at home. The oven floor provides the hottest, most even and direct heat possible, which means you can get your vegetables nice and caramelized without overcooking them.

Yogurt Green Goddess

A little yogurt turns a simple lemony vinaigrette into something totally original—and really flavorful. We used a similar vinaigrette in Nancy Silverton's *Mozza at Home*, which we were finishing up at the time I started working on this one. I had a jar of the dressing in my refrigerator and found myself drizzling it onto all kinds of salad and roasted vegetable bowls. Make this once and you'll see for yourself. *Makes about 2 cups*

½ cup packed fresh parsley leaves

2 tablespoons packed fresh sage

2 tablespoons packed fresh oregano (or marjoram)

2 tablespoons packed fresh thyme

2 tablespoons extra-virgin olive oil

1 cup plain Greek yogurt

¼ cup buttermilk (shake before pouring)

Juice of ½ lemon

1 garlic clove

½ teaspoon kosher salt

Put all the ingredients in a blender and blend until the dressing is light green. This dressing will keep, covered, for up to 3 days. (Try it as a dip for raw vegetables.)

SPICY TUNA TARTARE
with Brown Sushi Rice and Avocado

1 pound sushi-grade
ahi tuna

3 tablespoons low-sodium
soy sauce (or tamari)

2 tablespoons mirin
(Japanese sweet rice wine;
substitute dry sherry)

2 tablespoons fresh lemon
juice (or lime juice)

1 heaping tablespoon finely
chopped pickled ginger,
plus more for garnish

1 teaspoon kosher salt, plus
more for the avocados

1½ teaspoons toasted
sesame oil

½ teaspoon wasabi paste

½ cup mayonnaise

1 tablespoon Sriracha

Brown Sushi Rice (recipe
follows)

2 avocados, halved, pitted,
peeled, and thinly sliced

Toasted sesame seeds
(black, white, or a combo),
for sprinkling

3 scallions, white and light
green parts only, minced

1 to 2 cups radish sprouts
(or another type of sprouts
or microgreens)

Radishes for garnish
(optional)

I learned to make tuna tartare for a dinner I private-cheffed at the home of a legendary television director. His wife gave me a little leeway when it came to what entrées to serve, but for appetizers, she had a definite plan. She wanted guacamole, hummus, and Asian-style tuna tartare: three foods, from three different continents, that had probably never existed together on the same table until this dinner. I didn't love having to serve Around the World in Three Appetizers, but I welcomed the excuse to teach myself to make tuna tartare. I serve the tartare over sushi-style brown rice, so it's like a deconstructed spicy tuna roll. *Serves 4*

Set a timer for 10 minutes, start the timer, then put the tuna in the freezer. Take the tuna out the minute the timer goes off so you don't accidentally freeze the fish. (Chilling the fish firms it up and makes it easier to cut.)

While the fish is chilling, stir the soy sauce, mirin, lemon juice, ginger, salt, sesame oil, and wasabi paste together in a medium bowl. In a separate small bowl, stir the mayonnaise and Sriracha together.

Using the sharpest knife you have, cut the tuna into ¼-inch cubes. Here's how to do it without butchering the tuna: Slice the steak ¼ inch thick. Lay the slices flat, cut them into ¼-inch-wide strips, and then cut in the other direction to create ¼-inch cubes. Add to the bowl with the soy sauce mixture.

To serve, smear the spicy mayonnaise on the bottom of the bowls. Scoop the rice into the bowls, lay the avocado halves on top, and sprinkle them with salt. Spoon the tuna tartare on each serving and rain the sesame seeds, scallions, and sprouts over the whole pretty picture. Garnish with pickled ginger and radishes, if you're

using them. Serve with chopsticks, with forks as backup, so nobody has to stay frustrated for long.

Brown Sushi Rice

Makes about 3 cups

1 cup short-grain brown rice, rinsed

2 teaspoons kosher salt

¼ cup rice vinegar

1 tablespoon sugar (optional)

Combine the rice, 1 teaspoon of the salt, and 1¾ cups water in a saucepan and bring the water to a boil over high heat. Reduce the heat to low, cover, and simmer for 45 minutes, until the liquid has been absorbed. Remove from the heat, dump the rice onto a baking sheet, and spread it out to cool. (This takes the place of the sushi chef fanning it.)

Stir the vinegar, sugar (if you're using it), and the remaining 1 teaspoon salt together in a small bowl and drizzle over the cooled rice. Toss gently with a rubber spatula, taking care not to smash the rice.

MILLET POLENTA
with Wild Mushrooms and Parmesan

FOR THE POLENTA

2 tablespoons olive oil

2 teaspoons kosher salt

½ cup polenta (medium-ground cornmeal)

½ cup millet, rinsed

¼ cup finely grated Parmesan cheese, plus more for grating or sprinkling over the finished polenta

At some point early on in my journey of eating good to feel well, I made the mistake of looking at the back of a bag of polenta and discovered that, nutritionally speaking, polenta really has nothing going for it. What it does contain are calories, fat, and cholesterol, but since bulking up on nutrition-free carbs isn't really my thing, as much as I liked the warm, baby-food quality of polenta, I tried to steer clear of it. That is, until I discovered millet. When you cook them together, you get the corn flavor of polenta and the nutritional qualities of the millet. You can also use this polenta as a g-free base for your favorite meat sauce; or put an egg on it and call it breakfast. This is a vegetarian dish and gluten-free. *Serves 4*

FOR THE MUSHROOMS

1 pound mixed mushrooms (such as chanterelles, yellowfoot, trumpet, oyster, shiitake, matsutake, or cremini)

4 tablespoons (½ stick) unsalted butter

6 garlic cloves, smashed with the flat side of a knife

A small handful of fresh thyme sprigs

2 teaspoons kosher salt

For the polenta, bring 4 cups water to a boil in a small saucepan over high heat. Add the oil and salt and slowly rain in the polenta and millet, whisking continuously so they don't clump up. Reduce the heat and simmer, stirring often, until the grains are tender and thick like porridge, about 30 minutes. Turn off the heat and stir in the Parmesan. Leave the pot on the stove until you're ready to serve the polenta.

Meanwhile, to prepare the mushrooms, trim the tough ends from the stems of the mushrooms and wipe off any dirt with a wet paper towel.

Combine half the butter, half the garlic, and half the thyme sprigs in a large skillet and heat over medium heat until the butter melts and sizzles but doesn't brown, about 1 minute. Add half the mushrooms, sprinkle with 1 teaspoon of the salt, and give them a quick stir to distribute the salt. Spread the mushrooms out so they are lying flat in a single layer and cook until they are deep golden brown on both sides, transferring the garlic cloves and mushrooms from the pan to a plate as soon as they are golden brown on both sides. Remove the thyme sprigs and add them to the plate with their friends. Add the remaining butter, garlic, and thyme; the butter will melt almost immediately since the pan is already hot. Add the remaining mushrooms, sprinkle them with the remaining 1 teaspoon salt, and cook them as you did the first batch. Transfer the garlic, mushrooms, and thyme to the plate with the first batch.

If the polenta has cooled and thickened up, warm it over medium-low heat with enough water to bring it back to a loose, spoonable consistency. Spoon it into four wide-mouthed bowls. Pile the mushrooms, garlic, and thyme on top and sprinkle or grate Parmesan over the mushrooms so it looks like a light drift of fresh snow.

SALMON POKE BOWL
with Brown Rice and Edamame

12 ounces salmon fillet (or sushi-grade ahi tuna, or cooked shrimp)

½ cup canola oil (or another neutral-flavored oil)

½ cup rice vinegar (or white or red wine vinegar)

¼ cup low-sodium soy sauce or tamari

1 (2-inch) piece fresh ginger, peeled and grated on a Microplane or minced (about 2 teaspoons)

1 teaspoon kosher salt

2 red serrano or jalapeño chiles (preferably red), thinly sliced

1½ cups shelled edamame

1 bunch scallions, white and light green parts only, thinly sliced into rounds

1 cup long-grain brown rice, cooked (see page 36; about 3½ cups cooked rice)

Toasted sesame seeds (white, black, or a combination)

Poke is the definition of "clean" food—as long as you start with "clean" fish. Make this with the best quality fish you can get your paws on. You don't need me to tell you that an avocado would be welcome here, but trust me when I tell you that it's a completely delicious and compelling little bowl of edible glory without it. *Serves 4*

Set a timer for 10 minutes, start the timer, then put the salmon in the freezer. (This firms the fish, which makes it easier to cut.) Take the salmon out the minute the timer goes off so you don't accidentally freeze your fish.

While the salmon is in the freezer, combine the oil, vinegar, soy sauce, ginger, and salt in a large bowl.

Using the sharpest knife you have, cut the salmon into ¼-inch cubes. Here's how:

Cut the fish into ¼-inch-thick slices. Lay the slices flat, cut them into ¼-inch-wide strips, and then cut in the other direction to create ¼-inch cubes. Put the salmon cubes in the bowl with the oil and vinegar mixture. Add the chiles, edamame, and scallions and toss gently. Serve the poke over the rice and rain on the sesame seeds.

WARM CHICKEN CAESAR BOWL
with Quinoa and Kale

FOR THE CHICKEN

¼ cup fresh lime juice

2 tablespoons olive oil, plus more for cooking the chicken

2 skinless boneless chicken breast halves

1 teaspoon kosher salt

Freshly ground black pepper

FOR THE BOWLS

1 head curly kale

Caesar Dressing (recipe follows)

1 cup quinoa, cooked (see page 42; about 3½ cups cooked quinoa)

Freshly ground black pepper

Parmesan cheese for grating or sprinkling on top

I was born in Tijuana, where the Caesar salad was invented. My father owned a restaurant there in the 1960s, one block away from the Hotel Caesar, where he tossed the salad tableside with as much showmanship and panache as a handsome waiter could bring to the tossing of lettuce in a big wooden bowl. The salad is, in a way, my inheritance, and I have made it my mission to make the best Caesar salad on the planet. And I happen to think I've succeeded. The dressing is traditional, but for this bowl I use shredded kale instead of romaine.

Marinated for a short time, the chicken breasts defy their reputation for being dry and having no personality. They are moist and juicy. They are flavorful. And yet, they are still chicken breasts. It's almost a miracle. This bowl is g-free. *Serves 4*

For the chicken, combine the lime juice and olive oil in a glass or ceramic baking dish or bowl or in a zip-top plastic bag. Add the chicken breasts, turn to coat with the marinade, and cover the dish or close the bag. Put the chicken in the refrigerator to marinate for up to 2 hours; any longer and the lime juice will cook the chicken. Remove the chicken from the marinade and throw out the marinade and the bag, if you used one. Season with the salt and several turns of pepper.

Pour enough oil into a large skillet to coat it and heat the oil over medium-high heat until it is searing hot (it will slide like water in the pan) but not smoking, 2 to 3 minutes; the chicken should sizzle loudly when it touches the pan. Lay the chicken in the pan and cook until deep golden brown on the first side, about 3 minutes. Turn the chicken, reduce the heat to medium, and cook for about 5 minutes, until the chicken is cooked through (the

juices will run clear when the chicken is pierced with a small sharp knife and the chicken will register 165°F on an instant-read thermometer). Remove the chicken from the skillet and let it rest for 5 minutes before slicing it.

For the bowls, stack two kale leaves at a time and roll them lengthwise into a tight log. Cut across the log to thinly slice the leaves, stopping when you get to the stems, and discard the stems.

To assemble the bowls, smear a spoonful of Caesar dressing on the bottom of four wide bowls and spoon the quinoa into the bowls. Lay the chicken slices on the quinoa and paint them with the dressing.

Toss the remaining dressing with the kale, massaging the dressing into the leaves, and pile the kale on top of the bowls. Grind pepper and grate or sprinkle a light drift of Parmesan on each bowl.

recipe continues

Caesar Dressing

Makes about 1¾ cups

½ cup canola oil (or another neutral-flavored oil)

½ cup extra-virgin olive oil

3 tablespoons fresh lime juice

2 tablespoons red wine vinegar

½ teaspoon Worcestershire sauce (optional; use it if you have it)

2 or 3 dashes Tabasco (optional; use it if you have it)

1 (1½- to 2-ounce) can or jar of anchovies (8 to 11 anchovy fillets), anchovies removed from the oil and minced

1 egg yolk

1 teaspoon Dijon mustard

¾ cup finely grated Parmesan cheese (about 4 ounces)

½ teaspoon kosher salt

Freshly ground black pepper

1 garlic clove, grated on a Microplane or minced

Combine the canola oil and olive oil in a glass measuring cup or another vessel with a spout. Combine the lime juice, vinegar, Worcestershire sauce, and Tabasco in a separate vessel, ideally with a spout.

Choose a medium bowl that will be easy to whisk in, such as a slope-sided glass or stainless-steel bowl. Combine the anchovies, egg yolk, and mustard in the bowl. Start whisking, then add the oil to the bowl drop by drop, whisking constantly, until an emulsion forms (see Making an Emulsion, page 114). Continue adding the oil, drizzling now instead of adding the oil one drop at a time, until you've added all of the oil; when the oil and egg become so thick that it becomes difficult to whisk, whisk in a few drops of the lime juice mixture. When you've added all the oil and lime juice mixture, add the Parmesan, salt, a *lot* of pepper, and the garlic and stir to combine. Use the dressing or refrigerate, covered, for up to a week.

GLAZED PORK BELLY
with Ginger Scallion Rice and Pickled Vegetables

FOR THE PORK BELLY

1 tablespoon sugar

1 tablespoon kosher salt

½ teaspoon freshly ground black pepper

1 (3- to 4-pound) skinned pork belly

1 tablespoon balsamic vinegar

1 tablespoon sambal oelek (or another Asian chile garlic paste)

3 tablespoons honey

FOR THE BOWL

Ginger Scallion Rice (recipe follows; or 1 cup long-grain brown rice or quinoa, cooked, see page 36 or page 42; about 3½ cups cooked grains)

Pickled Vegetables (recipe follows)

4 medium-cooked eggs (see page 59; optional)

4 scallions, white and green parts, thinly sliced into rounds

1 to 2 cups radish sprouts (or other sprouts or microgreens)

One of the great differences between what healthy eating means today and what it meant when I was growing up in the 1970s and '80s, is that today, the same health foodies shooting fresh turmeric juice and going on raw food cleanses are also, in many instances, eating pork. Even pork *belly*. As the name implies, pork belly comes from the belly of the pig, which, like the belly of many humans, is the fattiest part of the animal. Since fat equals flavor, pork belly is the most flavorful cut of pork there is; it's what bacon is made of. Just remember to ask your butcher to skin the pork belly for you; it's not a fun task and requires some knife skills

If you are a lover of pork belly, you will be pleased to know just how easy it is to cook. The story goes more or less like this: Stick the pork belly in the oven and leave it there, untouched, until it's fork tender. The end. Okay, there is one more thing: To optimize the flavor and ensure the pork comes out moist and tender, the pork does need to sit in a dry brine (a combination of salt, sugar, and pepper that penetrates the meat) for a few hours; even better if you can let it sit there for a day. So plan ahead. *Serves 4*

To make the pork belly, mix the sugar, salt, and pepper in a baking dish wide enough to fit the pork belly. Sprinkle the rub over the pork belly and use the meat to mop up the rub left in the dish. Cover the dish tightly with plastic wrap and refrigerate for at least 2 hours and up to 24 hours.

Adjust the oven racks so one is in the middle position and preheat the oven to 450°F.

Put a wire rack on a rimmed baking sheet and put the pork belly fat-side up on the rack. (If you don't have a rack, just throw the belly directly on the pan; it'll sit in its own fat as the fat from the belly renders, or melts off, but it'll be fine.) Roast the belly for 45 minutes, basting with the fat that will accumulate on the baking sheet. Reduce the heat to 200°F and roast for 90 minutes more.

Meanwhile, stir the vinegar, sambal oelek, and honey together in a small bowl.

Take the pork belly out of the oven, brush the honey-sambal glaze on top, and return it to the oven for 15 minutes to bake the glaze onto the pork. Remove the pork from the oven, brush the remaining glaze on top, and let it rest for 10 minutes before slicing it. Slice the pork ½ to ¾ inch thick against the grain.

To serve, spoon the rice into a serving bowl. Lay the pork belly slices on top and top with the pickled vegetables, eggs (if you're using them), scallions, and sprouts.

recipe continues

Ginger Scallion Rice

A little effort goes a long way with this rice. Consider it an option for any Asian-ish bowl. You can make the same magic with a steaming pot of quinoa. *Makes about 3 cups*

1 cup long-grain brown rice (or red rice or black rice), rinsed

1 teaspoon kosher salt

1 (1-inch) piece fresh ginger, peeled and grated on a Microplane or minced (about 1 teaspoon)

3 scallions, white and light green parts only, sliced into thin rounds (about ¼ cup)

Combine the rice in a large saucepan with 1½ cups water and the salt. Bring the water to a boil over high heat. Reduce the heat to low, cover the pan, and simmer for 20 to 30 minutes, until the rice is tender and the liquid has been absorbed. Turn off the heat and let the rice rest, covered, for 5 to 10 minutes. Uncover, add the ginger and scallions, and use a fork to gently fluff the rice and distribute the ginger and scallions.

Pickled Vegetables

If you're pickle obsessed, make a big batch of these and keep them in a jar in the refrigerator. Serve them with any bowl or as part of a Build Your Own Spread with an Asian or Mexican vibe. They're sweet and acidic and crunchy, and you're going to love them. *Makes about 2 cups*

1 cup distilled white vinegar

3 tablespoons sugar

1 tablespoon kosher salt

2 bay leaves (preferably fresh)

1 tablespoon whole black peppercorns

2 garlic cloves, smashed

2 medium or large carrots, cut into matchsticks

3 radishes, trimmed, scrubbed, and quartered

3 medium shallots, peeled and quartered

Combine everything but the carrots, radishes, and shallots in a small saucepan. Add 1 cup water and bring the water to a boil to dissolve the sugar and salt. Put the carrots, radishes, and shallots in a heat-safe quart-size jar or other heatproof container and pour the pickling liquid over them. Let the vegetables sit in the pickling liquid for at least 1 hour before using them. Let them cool to room temperature, then cover and refrigerate until you're ready for them or for up to several weeks.

Build Your Own
Asian Bowl

PROTEINS
Glazed Pork Belly

Marinated Salmon, Shrimp, Chicken, or Tofu

Korean Short Ribs

Sambal Tofu

Five-Spice Riblets

GRAINS
Coconut Rice

Kimchi Rice

Ginger Scallion Rice

Plain Rice or Quinoa

VEGETABLES
Roasted Broccoli

Cucumber Salad

Shredded purple cabbage

Carrot ribbons

Fresh basil, mint, cilantro

Fresh lettuce leaves

Raw sugar snaps or snow peas

Bean sprouts

CONDIMENTS
Roasted salted peanuts or cashews

Peanut Sauce

Ponzu Sauce

Sweet Miso Dressing

Sweet and Tangy Vinaigrette

Low-sodium soy sauce or tamari

CHICKEN OR TOFU SATAY BOWL
with Coconut Rice

FOR THE SATAY

2 skinless boneless chicken breast halves or 4 skinless boneless chicken thighs; or 1 (12- to 16-ounce) package firm tofu, drained

¼ cup canned coconut milk

2 tablespoons fish sauce

1 tablespoon yellow curry powder

1 tablespoon coconut sugar (or raw or granulated sugar)

1 teaspoon kosher salt

Canola oil (or another neutral-flavored oil)

FOR THE SALAD

½ cup rice vinegar

1 tablespoon sugar

½ teaspoon kosher salt

2 Persian cucumbers, sliced ¼ inch thick

½ small red onion, thinly sliced into half-moons

1 Fresno or red or green serrano chile, stemmed and thinly sliced

FOR THE BOWLS

Thai Peanut Sauce (recipe follows)

Coconut Rice (recipe follows, or 1 cup red or brown rice, see page 42 or 36, cooked; about 3½ cups cooked grains)

In my hometown, San Diego, there is a takeout Thai barbecue place that offers an appealingly limited menu of roasted chicken on the bone, steamed red or white rice, a choice of cucumber or cabbage salad, and a selection of sauces. We get this often for family dinners when nobody wants to cook. It's like getting a bucket of KFC with sides, only with yummy Thai flavors and none of the nastiness of KFC. This is my bowl version of that barbecue. It's dairy- and g-free, and can even be vegan if you choose tofu. I just want you to be happy.

You will need 8 to 12 skewers for this recipe; if you're using wooden skewers, soak them in water for at least 10 minutes before using them. *Serves 4*

To make the satay, cut the chicken into 1-inch-wide strips, or slice the tofu ½ inch wide. Stir the coconut milk, fish sauce, curry powder, and sugar together in a ceramic or glass baking dish and add the chicken or tofu to the bowl. (If you are preparing both, divide the marinade; don't marinate chicken with other ingredients because of the dangers of salmonella.) Set aside to marinate for 15 minutes. Remove the chicken and/or tofu from the marinade, thread the slices onto the skewers, and season with the salt.

Meanwhile, to make the salad, stir the vinegar, sugar, and salt together in a large bowl. Add the cucumbers, onion, and chiles and stir to immerse them in the liquid.

To assemble the bowls, smear a big spoonful of peanut sauce on the bottom of four bowls. Pile the rice on top and set aside while you cook the satay.

Heat a cast-iron grill pan (or a skillet) over high heat and brush with the oil. Add the chicken or tofu until they have deep brown grill marks (or are caramelized) on both sides, about 3 minutes per side. Remove from the pan and put the satay on the patiently waiting bowls.

Mound the cucumber salad next to each serving of chicken and serve the remaining peanut sauce on the side.

Thai Peanut Sauce

For many years, peanut sauce was an unsolvable mystery. I tried bottled sauces, which taste nothing like the sauce we know and love from Thai restaurants. I made a few recipes, none of which compared. Finally, I resorted to stopping by my favorite Thai restaurants and buying a container of it. But that was then. I'm happy to report that with this recipe, the mystery has been solved. And the great news? It doesn't call for any wild and crazy ingredients. This recipe is designed to include the rest of the can of the coconut milk you used to make your satay.

Makes about 1½ cups

10 to 11-ounces canned coconut milk

¾ cup peanut butter (preferably chunky)

2 tablespoons coconut sugar (or raw or granulated sugar)

1½ tablespoons fish sauce

1 tablespoon finely grated yellow onion

2 garlic cloves, grated on a Microplane or minced

1 (2-inch) piece fresh ginger, peeled and grated on a Microplane or minced (about 2 teaspoons)

¼ teaspoon cayenne pepper, plus more to taste

Pinch of ground cumin (optional; use it if you have it)

Combine all the ingredients in a small saucepan and bring to a simmer over medium heat. Reduce the heat to low and simmer, stirring often, until the sauce is thick, about 10 minutes. Add more cayenne to taste. Turn off the heat and let the sauce cool to room temperature.

Store leftover sauce in the refrigerator for up to a week. It will thicken in the fridge, so before serving it, warm with a splash of water over low heat.

recipe continues

Coconut Rice

Coconut rice sounds great in theory but after making it twenty different ways, I discovered that coconut milk, because it has a lot of fat in it, makes rice heavy and gummy. I finally made a version using only a portion of coconut milk and adding flaky coconut at the end, which did the job of making it taste good and coconutty while still keeping the fluffy texture of a successful batch of rice. You know what they say: the twenty-first time is the charm. This makes a lot of rice because I wanted to utilize the whole can of coconut milk. Use leftovers for any Asian-ish bowl, or to make Quick and Easy Breakfast Fried Quinoa (page 53).

Makes about 6 cups

1 (15-ounce) can coconut milk, shaken

2 cups basmati rice (or another long-grain brown rice), rinsed

1½ teaspoons kosher salt

½ cup unsweetened shredded coconut

Combine the coconut milk, rice, salt, and 1½ cups water in a large saucepan and bring the liquid to a simmer over high heat. Reduce the heat to low, cover, and cook until the liquid has evaporated, 20 to 30 minutes. Turn off the heat and let the rice rest, covered, for 10 minutes. Add the shredded coconut and fluff it in with a fork so it makes friends with the rice while the rice is still warm.

SPICED RICE AND LENTILS
with Seared Halloumi

1 (8- or 9-ounce) package halloumi, drained (if packed in water, or panela), patted dry, and sliced into 8 slabs

Olive oil

2 cups loosely packed baby kale, or 1 bunch kale, stemmed, leaves torn into 1-inch pieces

Lemon Yogurt Dressing (page 94)

Spiced Rice and Lentils (recipe follows; or 1 cup long-grain brown rice, cooked, see page 36; about 3 cups cooked rice)

8 Slow-Roasted Tomato halves (page 56; or oil-packed sundried tomatoes)

¼ cup pine nuts, toasted (see page 69)

Halloumi is a semisoft, brined, Cyprian cheese (that means it's from Cyprus, an island floating between Lebanon, Turkey, and Syria) traditionally made from a mixture of goat's and sheep's milk. It has a high melting point which means it has to get hotter than your average cheese before it melts, so when you panfry or grill it, it gets golden and crispy on the outside, and gooey on the inside, but it still holds its shape rather than turning into a melted blob. Goat's- and sheep's-milk halloumi is also easy for the lactose-challenged to digest. Easily digestible cheese as a main course. What more could you want?

If you can't find halloumi, substitute panela cheese, available where Latin products are sold. And if you don't have time to slow roast the tomatoes for this, serve it with marinated sun-dried tomatoes or fresh tomatoes instead. This bowl is vegetarian and gluten-free.
Serves 4

Put the halloumi in a small, flat bowl or baking dish, cover with olive oil, and marinate while you prepare the rest of the components for the bowl or up to overnight.

Toss the kale with ¼ cup of the yogurt dressing.

Remove the cheese slabs from the oil. Pour enough of the marinating oil into a large skillet to coat the pan generously and heat the oil over high heat for 2 to 3 minutes until it slides like water in the pan and is sizzling hot but not smoking. Lay the cheese slabs in the pan and sear until the cheese is a deep, rich brown, turning to cook both sides, about 45 seconds per side.

Serve the cheese, salad, rice and lentils, tomatoes, and pine nuts in separate dishes, or arrange them in individual pretty bowls with the remaining yogurt dressing on the side.

recipe continues

Spiced Rice and Lentils

This blend of lentils and rice, called Mejadra, is typical in Middle Eastern cuisine. The best part is the rings of sautéed sweet onions tangled throughout. Use it as a base for any bowl with a Middle Eastern vibe, or just eat it as it is, topped with a dollop of yogurt, finely chopped fresh parsley, and a fried egg, if you're so inclined. *Makes about 4½ cups*

½ cup brown lentils, rinsed

1 tablespoon plus 2 teaspoons kosher salt

Olive oil

1 large yellow onion, thinly sliced into rounds

1 tablespoon whole coriander seeds

1 cup long-grain brown rice, rinsed

1 teaspoon ground allspice

Put the lentils in a small saucepan. Add enough water to cover by 2 inches and 1 tablespoon of the salt. Bring the water to a boil over high heat, reduce the heat to maintain a simmer and cook the lentils for 12 minutes. (They'll still be fairly hard; you'll continue to cook them with the rice.) Remove the lentils from the heat and drain.

Meanwhile, pour enough oil into a large straight-sided skillet to coat it. Add the onions and 1 teaspoon of the remaining salt and cook over medium heat, stirring, until the onions are golden brown and very soft, 10 to 15 minutes. Transfer the onions to a plate. Add the coriander seeds, reduce the heat to low, and toast for 1 minute, shaking the pan so they toast evenly. Add the rice, the remaining 1 teaspoon salt, and the allspice and toast the grains for 1 to 2 minutes, stirring often. Add the lentils and 2 cups water and bring the water to a boil over high heat. Cover, reduce the heat to low, and cook for 30 to 35 minutes, until the water has evaporated and the grains are cooked. Turn off the heat, and let the rice and lentils rest for 10 minutes. Uncover, add the onions, and use a fork to gently fold them in.

SUMMER CORN FARROTTO
with Brown Butter and Sweet Burst Tomatoes

5 ears corn, shucked, kernels cut from the cob, and cobs reserved

2 tablespoons unsalted butter

Olive oil

½ large Spanish yellow onion, finely chopped

1 teaspoon kosher salt

1 cup farro, rinsed

½ cup dry white wine

1 pint small sweet cherry tomatoes (such as Sungolds or Sweet 100s)

½ cup grated Parmesan cheese, plus more for grating or sprinkling over the finished dish

Handful of fresh green or opal (purple) basil leaves (the smaller the leaves, the better)

G-Free Alternative: To make this gluten-free, substitute long-grain brown rice for the farro. The rice will take more time to cook than the farro so you'll need more liquid; if you run out of corn stock, use water.

Farrotto is like risotto, but made with farro instead of *riso*, which is Italian for "rice." It's a traditional Italian dish, not a whole-grain stand-in for risotto. Since Italians cook for flavor, not for health, farrotto is delicious. And just *happens* to be healthy. This farrotto is cooked with stock made from corn cobs, which makes for an intense corn experience, and is also my way of making sure you don't try making this with frozen corn. Don't try. It's all about the corn, so if it's not corn season, make something else, such as Butternut Squash Risotto (page 149) or Millet Polenta with Wild Mushrooms and Parmesan (page 129). *Serves 4*

Put the corn cobs in a tall stockpot with an insert, if you have one, or in any large pot and add 10 cups water. Bring the water to a boil over high heat. Reduce the heat to maintain a simmer and cook for 45 minutes to 1 hour, until the liquid has reduced by half. Strain the stock or lift out the insert and discard the cobs.

Meanwhile, put 1 cup of the corn kernels in a blender or mini food processor, add a splash of the corn water, and puree, adding more water if necessary to get things moving. Set aside.

Choose the smallest saucepan you have, preferably one with a light-colored bottom to brown the butter in. Add the butter and heat over medium heat until it begins to bubble and spurt, 3 to 5 minutes. Cook the butter, swirling the pan so it cooks evenly, until the butter has a nutty, toasted aroma and is clear with brown specks (those are milk solids), about 5 minutes. Pour the butter into a small bowl, otherwise, the milk solids will burn from the heat of the pan and the butter will be bitter instead of yummy. Set aside.

Pour enough olive oil into a medium saucepan to coat it and heat the oil over medium heat for 1 minute just to warm it slightly. Add the onion and whole corn kernels, season with the salt, and cook until the onion is tender, about 6 minutes, stirring often so the vegetables don't brown. Add the farro and toast,

recipe continues

stirring often until the grains begin to crackle, about 3 minutes. Add the wine and simmer until the farro has drunk the wine, about 2 minutes. Increase the heat to medium-high and stir in the corn puree and a big ladleful (about 1 cup) of the corn stock. Cook, stirring often, until the farro has absorbed the liquid. Continue cooking the farro, adding the stock a ladle- or cupful at a time and allowing the grains to absorb the stock each time before adding more, until the farro is creamy and the grains are tender and have burst open, 45 minutes to 1 hour. Add ½ ladleful of stock and cook for a few minutes, until

the farrotto is a loose and spoonable consistency, like porridge, not so runny that you couldn't eat it with a fork. If the farrotto gets too dry, add more stock or water. Stir in the tomatoes and cook for a minute or two so the tomatoes burst slightly. Turn off the heat and stir in the brown butter and Parmesan.

Spoon the farrotto into four big shallow bowls and drop the small basil leaves (or snip larger leaves with scissors) over each portion. Serve more Parmesan for sprinkling or grating at the table.

BURNT VEGETABLE BOWL
with Black Rice and Lentils and Tahini Sauce

1 heaping tablespoon plus 1 heaping teaspoon kosher salt

½ cup beluga lentils (or French lentils), rinsed

1 cup black rice or black quinoa, cooked (see page 35 or 42; about 3½ cups cooked grains)

¼ cup plus 2 tablespoons extra-virgin olive oil

2 bunches Broccolini, trimmed of tough ends

8 ounces green beans or Romano beans, stem ends trimmed, tails left intact

8 ounces okra

3 medium zucchini (about 1 pound), sliced ¾ inch thick

Tahini Sauce (recipe follows)

Toasted sesame seeds (black or white or a combination), for sprinkling

In this recipe, vegetables are taken from the more common, yummy territory of caramelized to the brave new world of burnt. Burnt food is one of the latest, hottest trends in food, but more important, it tastes terrific. You get the sweet flavor of roasted vegetables with an added touch of smoky, fire flavor, and crispy burnt texture. I stick with the burnt color scheme and serve the vegetables with a mix of black grains and black lentils, called beluga lentils, which are tiny, shiny black lentils that look like caviar. (Get it? Beluga?)

In addition to the vegetables listed here, others that would benefit from a good burn are broccoli (cut into 1-inch-thick trees), Brussels sprouts, and asparagus, or any other sturdy green vegetable. Use a mix of vegetables or all of one. This is a vegan bowl and also g-free. This recipe makes a large quantity of the lentil-grain base. Put an egg on it and/or a dollop of yogurt and call it breakfast. *Serves 4*

Bring 3 cups water to a boil in a small to medium saucepan over high heat. Add 1 heaping tablespoon of the salt and the lentils, and return the water to a boil. Reduce the heat to maintain a gentle simmer and cook the lentils, uncovered, until they are tender but not falling apart, about 25 minutes. (If you boil the lentils over too high heat, they will split open and lose their beautiful black sheen.) Drain and transfer the lentils to a big bowl. Add the cooked grains, drizzle with 2 tablespoons of the oil, and toss with a rubber spatula, being careful not to smash the lentils.

Adjust the oven racks so none are near the oven floor; you will put the baking sheet on the oven floor. (If you have an oven where you can't use the oven floor, put one rack as close to it as possible.) Preheat the oven to 500°F.

Toss the vegetables in a large bowl with the remaining ¼ cup olive oil and the remaining heaping teaspoon of salt. Spread the vegetables out onto two large baking sheets, making sure the flat sides of the vegetables are touching the pan; the part that is touching the pan will burn, and burned is what we're going for. Put one baking sheet on the floor of the oven and roast until the bottom sides of the vegetables are burnt, 6 to 10 minutes, depending on your oven. Remove the baking sheet from the oven, turn the vegetables with tongs, and return them to the oven to blacken the second sides. Remove the baking sheet from the oven and repeat with the second batch of vegetables.

To serve, smear ¼ cup of the tahini sauce on the bottom of each of four bowls. Scoop a mound of the lentil and grain extravaganza into the bowl, arrange the vegetables on top, and sprinkle with the sesame seeds. Serve the rest of the tahini sauce on the side for dipping and drizzling.

recipe continues

Tahini Sauce

Tahini is sesame seed paste. You have to do very little to it to turn it into tahini sauce, which is a grain bowl's best condiment friend. Use this on any Middle Eastern-ish bowl, or in place of the Yogurt Green Goddess on the Farmers' Market Bowl (page 123). *Makes about 1 cup*

½ cup tahini (sesame seed paste)

3 tablespoons fresh lemon juice (from about 1 lemon)

1 garlic clove, grated on a Microplane or minced

¾ teaspoon kosher salt

Combine all the ingredients in a mini food processor or blender and pulse a few times. Add ½ cup water slowly through the feed holes in the top of the food processor until the sauce is smooth, adding more water until you achieve a loose drizzling consistency. The sauce will keep, refrigerated, for up to 1 week. It will thicken as it sits; bring it to room temperature and stir in enough water to bring it back to a drizzling consistency before you use it.

BUTTERNUT SQUASH RISOTTO
with Slow-Cooked Kale

FOR THE RISOTTO

2 tablespoons unsalted butter

1 large Spanish yellow onion, finely diced

1 small butternut squash (about 1½ pounds), halved, skin cut off with a large knife and discarded, and cut into ½-inch cubes (about 2 cups)

1 teaspoon kosher salt, plus more to taste

1 cup long- or short-grain brown rice, rinsed

½ cup dry white wine

8 cups chicken stock (preferably homemade, page 79; or sodium-free or low-sodium store-bought) or as needed

¼ cup grated Parmesan cheese, plus more for sprinkling or grating over the risotto

FOR THE KALE

Olive oil

1 large Spanish yellow onion, thinly sliced

1 árbol chile pod (or a pinch of red pepper flakes)

½ teaspoon kosher salt

2 bunches black kale (aka cavolo nero, dinosaur kale, or Tuscan kale), stemmed, leaves torn into large pieces

If I didn't tell you this was good for you—because it's made with brown rice and very little fat—you would never know. The kale is cooked low and slow until it's very dark, chewy, and so sweet it should be called "candied kale." I got the idea for cooking kale this way from the talented Los Angeles chef Suzanne Goin. Make this risotto in the wintertime, when you crave rich, warm foods. It's gluten-free and, except for the chicken stock, it's vegetarian. I use boxed chicken stock often, but I won't make this risotto unless I have or am willing to make chicken stock (page 79). I tried making it with both boxed chicken and vegetable stock, but the resulting risottos tasted like health food, and I don't mean that as a compliment. *Serves 4*

To prepare the risotto, melt the butter in a large straight-sided skillet. Add the onion and squash, sprinkle with the salt, and sauté over medium-low heat, stirring occasionally, for about 10 minutes, until the onion is translucent but not brown. (The squash will still be hard.) If the onion begins to brown, splash a bit of water or stock into the pan and lower the heat. Add the rice and stir with a wooden spoon or spatula until it is toasted and pearly looking, 2 to 3 minutes. Add the wine and cook for about 1 minute, until the rice has drunk the wine. Add 1 cup of stock and cook, stirring often, until the rice has absorbed the liquid. Continue in this way, adding the stock 1 cup at a time, and allowing the rice to absorb the stock each time before adding more, until the risotto is creamy and the rice is tender, about 1 hour. Add a big splash of stock and cook until the risotto is loose and soupy, like thick porridge that you could (and should) eat with a fork. If the risotto gets too dry, add more stock; if it's too runny, keep cooking. (You may not use all the stock; if,

on the other hand, you run out of stock, use water.) Turn off the heat and stir in the Parmesan. Taste for salt and add more if you think it needs it.

While the risotto is cooking, to prepare the kale, pour enough oil in a large skillet to generously coat it and heat the oil over medium heat for a minute or two, just to warm it slightly. Add the onion, chile, and salt and cook, stirring often so the onion doesn't brown, until soft, 6 to 8 minutes. Add the kale; it won't want to fit in the pan at first, but it will get more comfortable as it wilts. Reduce the heat to low and cook the kale, stirring occasionally so it cooks evenly, for about 20 minutes, until it is dark green and chewy.

Spoon the risotto into four big shallow bowls; soup or pasta bowls are ideal for this. Drop the kale on top of the risotto and grate a generous amount of Parmesan over each serving. Serve with more cheese at the table; you know you'll want it.

GRAVEYARD RICE
with Bone Marrow and Parsley Salad

FOR THE RICE

3 (cylindrical cut) marrow bones

2 medium or large shallots, minced

2 teaspoons kosher salt

1½ cups long-grain brown rice and wild rice mix

3¼ cups chicken stock, homemade (page 79; or sodium-free or low-sodium store-bought)

2 parsnips, scrubbed, halved lengthwise, and cut into 2 segments

6 to 8 baby turnips, scrubbed and halved

FOR THE SALAD

1 bunch fresh flat-leaf parsley

Long strips of zest from 2 lemons

Juice of ½ lemon

1 tablespoon extra-virgin olive oil

Maldon, fleur de sel, or another flaky sea salt (or kosher salt)

Bone marrow, a fatty substance found inside bones, is considered a delicacy. Roasted bone marrow is having a renaissance as Americans are becoming more daring about what they eat, but chances are, many of them have been eating bone marrow and not knowing it, as it's the base of Vietnamese pho, and also of traditional Italian veal osso buco. In this recipe, bone marrow turns a simple pot of rice into something totally decadent and special. I call it "graveyard rice," because it reminds me of a bunch of bones in a graveyard, what with the white veggies and the actual bones.

You will need to use a sauté pan that is at least as deep as the marrow bone is tall so the lid will fit tightly. Alternatively, cover the pan tightly with aluminum foil. *Serves 4*

To prepare the rice, put the marrow bones cut-side down in a large sauté pan and cook over medium-low heat for about 15 minutes, turning the bones to render (melt) the marrow from each side; you may need to reach inside the cavities of the bones with a small spoon or paring knife to get all the marrow out. Add the shallots, sprinkle with ½ teaspoon of the salt, and sauté over medium-low heat, stirring so they don't brown, until they're soft, about 4 minutes. Add the rice and the remaining 1½ teaspoons salt and toast the rice in the fat for a minute or two. (If you use chicken stock that contains salt, only add ½ teaspoon salt.) Add the stock, increase the heat to high, and bring the stock to a simmer. Reduce the heat to low, cover, and cook for 10 minutes. Remove the lid, scatter the parsnips and turnips over the surface of the rice, and cover. Simmer the rice and vegetables, covered, for about 40 minutes, until the liquid has been absorbed. Turn off the heat and let the rice and vegetables rest, covered, for 10 minutes before serving.

To prepare the salad, toss the parsley, lemon zest strips, lemon juice, olive oil, and a big pinch of salt in a bowl.

Serve family style, or spoon the rice and vegetables into four bowls and top each with a big tangle of the parsley salad.

Build Your Own Farmers' Market–Inspired Bowl

PROTEINS

Grilled Chicken

Poached Salmon

Medium-Cooked Eggs

GRAINS

Quinoa, sorghum, wild rice, or a mix of all three

Farro, freekeh, or bulgur

Black rice with black lentils

VEGETABLES

Sliced radicchio

Shaved fennel

Shaved or spiralized zucchini

Blanched asparagus

Blanched green beans

Roasted vegetables (carrots, acorn squash, cauliflower, romanesco, beets, Brussels sprouts)

Grilled corn, tomatoes, zucchini, eggplant

Baked sweet potatoes

Radishes

Avocados

CONDIMENTS

Yogurt Green Goddess

Spicy Pepitas

Kale Pistachio Pesto

Hummus or Beet Hummus

Mozzarella, burrata, or goat cheese

Bagna Cauda

Toasted walnuts, almonds, pistachios, or pepitas

CHINO RANCH VEGETABLE BOWL
with Kale Pistachio Pesto and Bagna Cauda

2 red or yellow bell peppers (or 1 pound mini sweet peppers)

2 ears corn, shucked

½ pound Romano beans, green beans, or yellow beans, stem ends trimmed

1 bunch asparagus, tough ends snapped off

1 pint small cherry tomatoes, such as Sweet 100s, Sungolds, or another sweet summertime variety

Olive oil

Kosher salt and freshly ground black pepper

Kale Pistachio Pesto (recipe follows)

Bagna Cauda (recipe follows; optional)

1 cup farro, cooked (see page 37; about 3 cups cooked farro) and cooled to room temperature

8 ounces fresh mozzarella, sliced, or burrata, broken into segments with a spoon

½ cup fresh basil

G-Free Alternative: To make this gluten-free, substitute cooked sorghum, quinoa, or wild rice (or a combo) for the farro in the recipe.

Chino Ranch is a farm in my hometown, San Diego, made famous in the early 1970s when Alice Waters fell in love with their green beans because, unlike grocery store green beans, they actually had tasted like green beans. Extraordinary as those beans are, the Chinos are most famous for their corn, which, were you to try it, will ruin you to any other corn for life. I am lucky enough to call the Chinos friends, and to have easy access to their delicious vegetables. Naturally, I serve many a bowl in honor of them and their ever-changing, unparalleled produce.

Pesto is so easy to make I can't understand why anyone would buy it. You just throw a bunch of stuff in a blender or food processor and go. Try it, you'll see. I make this with kale but use any combination of basil, parsley, kale, or arugula; as long as you start with 2 cups of leaves, you'll have pesto. *Serves 4 to 6*

Preheat an outdoor grill to high or a stovetop grill pan over high heat. Brush the vegetables with olive oil and season with salt and black pepper. Put the vegetables on the grill and grill until they are black in places, turning to grill all sides, and removing each vegetable from the grill to a plate as it is done. (For bright green asparagus and green beans like those pictured rather than grilling them, blanch them for 1 minute in boiling, salted water and immediately plunge them into a bowl of ice water to stop the cooking process.)

Cut the corn kernels off the cob. Remove and discard the cores and seeds from the bell peppers (if you used baby peppers, leave them as is) and slice the peppers into thin strips.

Serve family style, with big platters of the summer veggies, the sauces in small bowls, and the grains for people to make their own bowls.

recipe continues

Kale Pistachio Pesto

Makes about 2 cups

1½ cups packed torn kale leaves

½ cup packed fresh parsley or basil leaves

½ cup extra-virgin olive oil, plus more as needed

¼ cup finely grated Parmesan cheese

2 tablespoons pistachios (or pine nuts, almonds, or walnuts), toasted (see page 69)

2 garlic cloves

1 teaspoon kosher salt

Juice of 1 lemon

Put all the ingredients except the lemon juice in a blender or food processor and blend until the pesto is smooth with some flecks, stopping to scrape down the side of the blender once or twice. The pesto should be loose and spoonable, not globby; if it's too thick, add more oil and blend it in. Stir in the lemon juice just before using. Use the pesto or refrigerate in a covered container for up to 2 days; be warned: the pesto will lose its pretty color with time but it will still taste great. Bring it to room temperature before using.

Bagna Cauda

Bagna cauda means "warm bath" in Italian. It's a simple condiment made of anchovies, garlic, and olive oil. It turns something as simple as blanched, veggies into something totally special and delicious. Drizzle it on blanched or roasted asparagus, green beans, Broccolini, cauliflower, or sweet peppers.

Makes about ¼ cup

¼ cup plus 2 tablespoons extra-virgin olive oil

6 tablespoons unsalted butter

1 (1½- to 2-ounce) can or jar of anchovies (8 to 11 anchovy fillets), anchovies removed from the oil and minced

6 garlic cloves, grated on a Microplane or minced

A pinch of red pepper flakes (optional)

A few turns of freshly ground black pepper

Combine all the ingredients in a small saucepan and heat over medium heat until the garlic is fragrant and the butter and oil just start to sizzle. Reduce the heat to very low and cook for 10 minutes so the flavors can all make friends. Serve warm.

MOROCCAN MILLET
with Braised Root Vegetables and Harissa

16 fresh pearl onions, trimmed of root ends (or frozen pearl onions)

2 pounds mixed parsnips, turnips, carrots, and rutabaga

1 bunch radishes

1 tablespoon kosher salt

2 bay leaves (preferably fresh)

4 thyme sprigs (optional; use them if you have them)

1½ cups cooked chickpeas (page 104), or 1 (15-ounce) can, drained and rinsed

1 tablespoon unsalted butter

1 teaspoon sugar (optional)

Moroccan Millet (recipe follows)

Harissa (or another red pepper paste)

As much as I love roasted root vegetables, braising them is my favorite new discovery. Braised, the veggies don't shrivel up. Instead, they're tender and plump and creamy. And if you've never had cooked radishes, you will now. And you're in for a great surprise.

I use the trimmings from the vegetables to make a quick stock, which takes an hour too make; if you want to skip this step, use homemade chicken stock (page 79) or water. Made with commercial stock, the vegetables are, let's say, not amazing. Other than a tablespoon of butter, which is added at the end to give the veggies a yummy glazed finish, this dish is gluten-free and vegetarian. To make it vegan, skip the butter. *Serves 4*

Bring 4 cups water to a boil in a large saucepan over high heat.

If you're using frozen onions, skip this step: Fill a bowl with ice and cold water to make an ice bath. Put the onions in a strainer and plunge the strainer into the boiling water for 2 minutes. Lift the strainer out of the boiling water and plunge the onions in the ice water to stop them from cooking. Turn the onions out onto a clean towel to dry and slip off and discard the peels. Reserve the water in the saucepan.

Trim and peel the parsnips, turnips, carrots, and rutabaga, and cut them into 1- to 1½-inch pieces. Trim and scrub the radishes and cut them in half. Add the vegetable trimmings and peelings to the saucepan of water and bring the water to a simmer over high heat. Reduce the heat to maintain a simmer and cook the liquid for 45 minutes to 1 hour to make a light vegetable stock. Turn off the heat. Strain the stock and discard the solids in the strainer.

Put all the vegetables in a large straight-sided skillet or Dutch oven. Add the salt, bay leaves, and thyme (if you are using it). Add enough stock to come halfway up the side of the vegetables. Bring it to a boil over high heat, cover the pan, and reduce the heat to medium-low. Simmer the vegetables until they're tender when pierced with a fork but still hold their shape, about 40 minutes. Uncover and add the chickpeas, butter, and sugar (if you're using it). Baste the vegetables and chickpeas with the juices in the pan and cook over medium-high heat for 2 to 3 minutes, until the liquid has thickened and the vegetables are shiny and glazed.

To serve, pile the millet into four wide bowls. Spoon the vegetables with their juices over the millet and serve with the harissa on the side.

recipe continues

Moroccan Millet

This millet is cooked with carrot juice, bay leaf, and cinnamon stick so it has a beautiful golden color and unique, North African–like flavor. If you wanted to skip the carrot juice, cook it with water; the bay and cinnamon are what really give it a unique flavor. Serve leftover millet for breakfast with a fried egg and a dollop of yogurt, or add roasted carrots, toasted almonds, and fresh cilantro for a take-to-work lunch. *Makes about 4 cups*

2 tablespoons olive oil

½ medium Spanish yellow onion, finely chopped

2 bay leaves (preferably fresh)

1 cinnamon stick

1 teaspoon kosher salt

1 cup hulled millet, rinsed

1¾ cups fresh carrot juice (or water)

Adjust the oven racks so one is in the middle position and preheat the oven to 350°F.

Combine the oil, onion, bay leaves, cinnamon stick, and salt in a large ovenproof sauté pan (FYI: most sauté pans are ovenproof, even those with rubber handles) with a tight-fitting lid. Cook over medium heat, stirring often so the onion doesn't brown, for about 5 minutes, until the onion is soft and translucent. Add the millet and toast, stirring so it doesn't burn, for 2 minutes. Stir in the carrot juice, increase the heat to high, and bring to a boil. Turn off the heat and cover the pan. Put the pan in the oven for 25 to 30 minutes, until the millet has absorbed all the liquid. Remove the millet from the oven and let it sit, covered, for 10 minutes. Uncover, gently fluff with a fork, and be prepared to welcome millet into your heart.

FIVE-SPICE RIBLETS
with Sticky Rice and Apple Slaw

1 rack baby back ribs, sawed in half down the middle into riblets

½ cup apple cider vinegar

¼ cup Dijon mustard

¼ cup sambal oelek (or another Asian chile garlic paste)

½ cup maple syrup

½ cup molasses

½ teaspoon five-spice powder

2 teaspoons kosher salt

Sticky Rice and Apple Slaw (recipe follows)

Toasted white sesame seeds, for sprinkling

I call these ribs "candied meat" because they're so sticky and sweet. I adapted the recipe from one my friend Susan Spungen, who worked for *Martha Stewart Living* for years (and who also beautifully styled the food in this book), published in one of the books she did with Martha.

Have your butcher split the ribs down the middle so you can make bite-size riblets. If you buy your ribs at the grocery store with no butcher to be seen, it won't be the end of the world—you'll just have longer ribs to gnaw on. I serve the riblets with a refreshing rice and apple slaw, but if you prefer a hot entrée, serve them over Ginger Scallion Rice (page 135) or plain brown rice and a green vegetable. This bowl is the perfect example of serving meat as a side dish. *Serves 4*

Cut between each bone to create individual riblets.

Combine the vinegar, mustard, sambal, ¼ cup of the maple syrup, and ¼ cup of the molasses in a glass or ceramic baking dish or zip-top bag. Add the ribs and turn to coat them with the marinade. Cover the baking dish or close the bag and put the ribs in the refrigerator to marinate for at least 1 hour and as long as overnight.

Adjust the oven racks so one is in the middle position and preheat the oven to 350°F. To make easy cleanup, line a baking dish with aluminum foil. Make sure there are no tears or open seams in the lining; otherwise, the sticky stuff will leak onto the baking dish, which will cause the foil to stick to it.

Remove the ribs from the marinade and put them bone-side down on the foil-lined baking sheet. Pour the marinade over them and season the sides facing up with the five-spice powder and salt. Cover the pan tightly with foil and bake the ribs for 1¼ hours. While the ribs are cooking, stir the remaining ¼ cup maple syrup and

molasses together in a small bowl. Remove the ribs from the oven and remove the foil; be careful, as steam will rise from the pan.

Increase the oven temperature to 400°F.

Baste the ribs with the maple-molasses mixture and return them to the oven, uncovered. Bake until they are sticky and glazed looking, turning the ribs with tongs to coat them in the liquid a few times during the process; this will take anywhere from 10 to 30 minutes, depending on how much liquid is in the pan. Keep an eye on it, as the liquid can go from sticky and delicious to burnt pretty quickly.

To serve, pile the slaw into four or more bowls. Remove the ribs from the oven and serve them piled up on the bowls of slaw. Sprinkle the ribs with sesame seeds and serve.

recipe continues

Sticky Rice and Apple Slaw

Who doesn't love a good slaw? This one contains sticky rice, so it does double duty as a grain base for yummy sticky ribs, and a salad. It requires a lot of slicing. If you've been meaning to buy a mandoline, now is the time. *Serves 4 to 6*

½ cup canola oil

½ cup apple cider vinegar

2 tablespoons honey

2 teaspoons toasted sesame oil

1 teaspoon kosher salt

⅔ cup short-grain brown rice, cooked (see page 36; about 2 cups cooked rice)

½ head napa or green cabbage, cored and thinly sliced (about 4 cups)

1 cup sugar snap peas (or snow peas), very thinly sliced on an angle

4 radishes, trimmed, scrubbed, and cut into thin matchsticks

1 Granny Smith apple, halved, cored, and cut into thin matchsticks

1 (3- or 4-ounce) package pea shoots or pea shoot flowers (available at grocery stores), stems pinched off (optional)

2 tablespoons toasted sesame seeds (white, black, or both)

Combine the canola oil, vinegar, honey, sesame oil, and salt in a small jar, close the jar, and shake it vigorously to combine. (Alternatively, whisk everything together in a small bowl.)

Put the rice in a big bowl. Add the cabbage, sugar snap peas, radishes, apple, pea shoots, and sesame seeds. Drizzle half the dressing over the slaw and toss to mix everything together. Add more dressing if you think the slaw needs it.

COCONUT CURRY RICE BOWL
with Green Vegetables and Sweet Potatoes

Coconut oil (or canola oil)

¼ cup Thai green curry paste (such as Thai Kitchen or Mae Ploy brand)

1 (15-ounce) can coconut milk, shaken

1 cup chicken stock, homemade (page 79) or sodium-free or low-sodium store-bought or water

1 lemongrass stalk, smashed with the flat side of a large knife (optional)

2 tablespoons fish sauce

2 teaspoons raw, granulated, or coconut sugar

1 medium purple or yellow sweet potato, peeled and cut into ½-inch rounds

6 ounces Brussels sprouts (or broccoli florets, or a combination)

2 heads baby bok choy, halved lengthwise, or 1 head bok choy, quartered lengthwise

1 bunch kale, collard greens, or Swiss chard, stemmed, leaves torn into bite-size pieces

2 serrano, Fresno, or jalapeño chiles, very thinly sliced into rounds

Small handful of fresh basil (preferably Thai basil)

1 cup long-grain brown rice, cooked (or Ginger Scallion Rice or Coconut Rice see page 36, 135, or 140; about 3½ cups cooked rice)

Thai curry paste is the best thing to happen to the hurried home cook since prewashed greens. All that mysterious and wonderful Thai curry flavor, distilled into a small affordable jar that you can find on the shelves of even the most unremarkable supermarkets. You need coconut milk and fish sauce to complete the magic, so if you keep those in your pantry, you're just one fresh vegetable away from a warm and tasty last-minute meal. This is dairy-free and vegan if you use water in place of chicken stock. If you wanted to add protein, add 1 boneless skinless chicken breast half, cut into ½-inch cubes, and cook it in the curry for 5 minutes before serving. *Serves 4*

Coat a large saucepan or straight-sided skillet with oil. Add the curry paste and cook over medium heat for 1 minute, stirring continuously, to release the flavors. Stir in the coconut milk, stock, lemongrass (if you're using it), fish sauce, and sugar and bring the liquid to a simmer. Add the sweet potatoes and Brussels sprouts, reduce the heat to maintain a simmer, and cook for about 15 minutes, until the potatoes and Brussels sprouts are tender. Add the bok choy and kale and simmer for 2 to 3 minutes more to wilt them. Turn off the heat, remove and discard the lemongrass, if you used it. Throw in the chiles and basil, and serve the curry over the rice.

POMEGRANATE TABBOULEH
with Crunchy Falafel, Baba-G, and Tahini Sauce

FOR THE FALAFEL

½ pound (1 cup) dried chickpeas, soaked overnight and drained

½ small Spanish yellow onion, coarsely chopped

4 garlic cloves

¼ cup fresh parsley

2 tablespoons fresh cilantro

1 tablespoon kosher salt, plus more as needed

½ teaspoon ground cumin

½ teaspoon ground coriander

¼ teaspoon freshly ground black pepper

⅛ teaspoon ground cardamom (optional; if you have it, use it)

½ cup sparkling mineral water

½ teaspoon baking soda

2 to 3 cups canola oil (or another neutral-flavored oil), or as needed, for frying

FOR THE BOWLS

Pomegranate Tabbouleh (recipe follows)

Baba-G (recipe follows) or store-bought baba ghanoush

Tahini Sauce (page 148)

1 pint cherry tomatoes, halved and lightly salted (optional)

G-Free Alternative: To make this g-free, sub quinoa for the freekeh in the tabbouleh. It won't be as flavorful, but good health, like happiness, so often comes at the hands of compromise.

My friend Nancy Silverton went to Israel last year and came home with a rough, scribbled-down secret "recipe" for how to make what she promised were falafel so crispy, crunchy, and flavorful that they turned her, a falafel skeptic, into a believer. The first time I looked at it, I thought there was something wrong or missing from the recipe. If I'd been locked in a room until I could figure out what falafel was made of, I would have died an old woman before I would have guessed that those light and crunchy balls of savory, goodness were made from ground, *uncooked* chickpeas. Yes, the chickpeas *are* soaked, but they're still hard as rocks, and it's still amazing. Sparkling mineral water is supposedly the key to making these as crispy as they, in fact, turned out to be. The chickpeas must soak overnight, so plan ahead because this here is the one place in life where you can't substitute canned chickpeas. *Makes 18 to 20 falafel; serves 4 to 6*

To prepare the falafel, combine the chickpeas, onion, garlic, parsley, cilantro, salt, cumin, coriander, pepper, and cardamom (if you're using it) in a food processor and pulse until the chickpeas are finely ground. Turn the mixture out into a bowl and stir in the mineral water and baking soda. Cover the bowl and refrigerate for 1 hour to soften the ground chickpeas.

Pour 3 to 4 inches of canola oil into a small saucepan. Fasten a candy or deep-fry thermometer to the side of the saucepan or drop in an unpopped kernel of popcorn into the oil. Heat the oil over medium-high heat until the thermometer registers 350°F or the kernel pops. Remove the popcorn kernel if you used it. (I learned this trick from the venerable cooking magazine *Cooks Illustrated*, a great magazine if you want to learn to be a better or more knowledgeable cook.)

While the oil is heating, give the falafel mixture a good stir and scoop it into 1-ounce (2-tablespoon) portions; roll into balls, and put the balls on a baking sheet or plate. The mixture is very wet and can be awkward to work with; the moisture is what makes the falafels as light as they are.

Carefully drop the balls in the oil, adding only as many as will fit in a single layer, and fry them for 1 to 2 minutes, until they are golden brown and crispy, turning them as they cook so they brown evenly. Using a slotted spoon or strainer, transfer the falafel to paper towels to drain, and sprinkle with salt. Fry the rest of the falafel.

Serve the tabbouleh, baba-g, falafel, tahini sauce, and tomatoes (if you're serving them) family style or compose four to six bowls using those components.

recipe continues

Pomegranate Tabbouleh

Fresh pomegranates make a short appearance in stores during the fall and winter. They're so pretty that I buy enough to fill my favorite bowl so they can just sit and please me with their rustic, ruby-red beauty until I'm ready to eat them. When pomegranates aren't in season, use small cherry or grape tomatoes in their place. The tabbouleh makes a refreshing salad on its own, as well as a delicious base for Pomegranate-Glazed Lamb Meatballs (page 183) and Seared Halloumi (page 141). *Makes about 4 cups*

⅔ cup freekeh or bulgur, cooked (see page 38 or 37; about 2 cups grains), cooled to room temperature

½ cup finely chopped fresh parsley

½ cup finely chopped fresh mint

2 Persian cucumbers (or 1 hothouse or English cucumber), cut into ¼-inch cubes

Seeds from 1 large pomegranate (about 1 cup; or 1 pint small cherry tomatoes, halved)

½ cup extra-virgin olive oil

Juice of 2 lemons

2 teaspoons kosher salt

Put the freekeh in a big, wide bowl. Add the rest of the ingredients and toss everything up.

SEEDING A POMEGRANATE

The best way I know to remove pomegranate seeds from the fruit is one I learned only recently from the farmer and agriculture guru Tom Chino. Here's how he taught me to do it: Cut the skin of the fruit in half, then twist the pomegranate to break it in two. With the open side facing a bowl, spank the skin side of one pomegranate half with the biggest and heaviest wooden spoon you have; the seeds will pop right out of the fruit and into the bowl. Do this to the other half. If there are any stubborn seeds remaining in the shell that you're dying to salvage, put on a pair of kitchen gloves and dig them out with your fingers. (Some trick that is, right?) Pick out and discard any pulpy bits that might have ended up in the bowl with your seeds and move on with your recipe.

Baba-G

I love baba ghanoush but I don't like trying to spell it, so I call it by its yogi name, Baba-G. Charring eggplant directly on the burner of my gas stove is a technique I learned from the Israeli chef Yotam Ottolenghi, author of the brilliant book *Plenty*. If you don't have a gas stove (or don't want to make a mess), char the eggplants in a 450°F oven, on a grill, or under a broiler.

Makes about 2 cups

3 medium eggplants (about 3 pounds)

¼ cup tahini (sesame seed paste)

Juice of 1 lemon

1½ teaspoons kosher salt

2 garlic cloves, grated on a Microplane or minced

One at a time, cook the eggplants directly over a medium to high flame of a gas stove, turning them with tongs so they cook evenly, until they are charred all over and soft inside, about 10 minutes. Remove the eggplant from the heat and let it cool to room temperature. Cut the eggplants in half and scoop the flesh out into a mini food processor or a blender. Throw out the charred remains. Add the tahini, lemon juice, salt, and garlic and pulse to combine the ingredients; you want the finished baba-g to have some lumps and bumps, so stop the machine before it's completely smooth. Serve or refrigerate for up to several days; the baba-g will taste best if you have the restraint to bring it to room temperature before eating it.

Build Your Own
Middle Eastern Bowl

PROTEINS

Pomegranate-Glazed Lamb Meatballs

Crunchy Falafel

Seared Halloumi

Chickpeas

GRAINS

Spiced Rice and Lentils

Pomegranate Tabbouleh

Bulgur or freekeh

Black lentils with freekeh or black rice

Brown rice

VEGETABLES

Slow-Roasted Tomatoes

Tzatziki

Hummus

Baba-G

Sliced cherry tomatoes

Sliced cucumbers

Kale or spinach

Braised Root Vegetables

Fresh parsley and mint

CONDIMENTS

Seasoned Yogurt

Yogurt Vinaigrette

Tahini Sauce

Harissa

MOLE TEFF AND CHICKEN
with Avocado and Crema

FOR THE CHICKEN

2 cups chicken stock, homemade (page 79) or sodium-free store-bought

¼ cup Doña María Mole paste (from a glass jar)

6 bone-in, skin-on chicken thighs

2 teaspoons kosher salt

Canola oil (or another neutral flavored oil)

FOR THE TEFF

¼ cup Doña María Mole paste

1 teaspoon kosher salt

½ cup teff

FOR THE BOWLS

1 ripe avocado, quartered, pitted, and peeled

1 lime, halved

Kosher or sea salt

4 tablespoons Mexican crema or sour cream thinned with water or milk to a drizzling consistency

Toasted white sesame seeds, for sprinkling

1 white onion, thinly sliced into rounds or half-moons

Mole poblano is a Mexican sauce made of ground chiles, nuts, and chocolate, among a long list of other ingredients. Very few people make their own; even in Mexico, it's completely respectable to start with a bottle of Doña María (available at grocery stores), as this recipe calls for. Chicken with mole is a classic, but the way it's usually served—with the sauce blanketing a dry, flavorless chicken breast—leaves a lot to be desired. In this recipe, chicken thighs are braised in mole and then shredded with the braising liquid, so the end product is like the mole version of shredded barbecue chicken. It's the best chicken mole I've ever had, in my humble opinion. I garnish it exactly the way I would if I were making a traditional mole dish: with avocado, crema, white onion, and toasted sesame seeds and serve them on the mole left base.

If you're intrigued by the mole but you don't eat animals, replace the mole chicken with the mushrooms from the Millet Polenta (page 129).

For a more mainstream mole bowl, serve the chicken and toppings on a bowl of plain brown rice or quinoa. *Serves 4*

To prepare the chicken, adjust the oven racks so one is in the middle position and preheat the oven to 350°F.

Combine the stock and mole in a bowl. Smash and stir the mole with a whisk or fork to break it up and dissolve it. Season the chicken with the salt.

Coat a Dutch oven or ovenproof skillet with oil and heat the oil over medium-high heat until it slides like water in the pan and is sizzling hot but not smoking, 2 to 3 minutes. Add the chicken thighs, skin-side down, and cook until they are deep brown, about 5 minutes. Turn the chicken and cook for 2 minutes on the second side. Pour the mole-stock mixture around the chicken, adding enough so it comes halfway up the chicken; you may not use all the stock mixture. (Throw it out or use it in place of some of the water to make the teff.) Cover the pot and put the chicken in the oven to cook for about 1½ hours, until it is fork tender. (Stick a fork in a thigh and twist; the meat is done when the fork turns easily.) Remove the pot from the oven, uncover, and let the chicken rest in the liquid until it's cool enough to handle. Shred the chicken into a small saucepan; throw out the skin and bones. Skim the fat off the braising liquid with a spoon or ladle, discard the fat, and pour the remaining liquid into

recipe continues

the saucepan with the chicken. Bring the liquid to a simmer over high heat. Reduce the heat to maintain a simmer and cook the chicken and sauce together until the sauce has reduced and the chicken and sauce are one, about 10 minutes.

To prepare the teff, combine the mole, salt, and 2½ cups water in a small saucepan. Smash and stir the mole with a whisk to break it up and dissolve it. Bring the liquid to a boil over high heat. Rain in the teff, stirring with the whisk as you add it. Reduce the heat to low, cover the pan, and simmer until the grains are tender and thick, like loose polenta or porridge, about 30 minutes.

To assemble the bowls, season the avocado with the juice of the lime and salt. Spoon the teff into four serving bowls and pile the shredded chicken on top. Put the avocados on top of the chicken. Garnish with the crema, sesame seeds, and onion slices.

CHILE EN NOGADA BOWL
with Turkey Picadillo and Walnut Crema

FOR THE PICADILLO

½ cup golden raisins

1 cup fresh orange juice

Canola oil (or another neutral-flavored oil)

1 large Spanish yellow onion, finely chopped

1 bay leaf (preferably fresh; optional; use it if you have it)

1 árbol chile pod (or ¼ teaspoon chili powder)

2 teaspoons kosher salt, plus more as needed

4 garlic cloves, grated on a Microplane or minced

1 tablespoon double-concentrated tomato paste (from a tube) or 2 tablespoons regular tomato paste

2 pounds ground dark meat turkey

1 teaspoon ground cinnamon, plus more as needed

1 (15-ounce) can pureed tomatoes (preferably fire-roasted)

5 cups chicken stock, homemade (page 79) or sodium-free or low-sodium store-bought, or as needed

½ cup slivered almonds, toasted (see page 69)

ingredients continue

Chiles en Nogada, or "chiles in nut sauce," is a classic Mexican dish consisting of roasted poblano chilies stuffed with picadillo, a spiced ground meat mixture, and topped with walnut cream sauce and pomegranate seeds. Picadillo is generally made with ground pork, but this version is made with ground dark meat turkey, which is less dry than white meat and a lot more flavorful. I've tried making this with white meat and all I can say about that is "yikes!" While dark meat picadillo is so flavorful it's practically impossible to stop eating, the white meat version was so bland and dry I couldn't give it away. Use dark meat.

Pomegranate seeds are in season only for a short time in the fall and early winter. If you can't find them, skip them. I make a nut cream from ground walnuts, which makes this dairy-free. If you want to skip that step and dairy isn't an issue, plop some sour cream on top of the meat and call it a day.

I make a big batch when I make picadillo, because I love leftovers. My favorite way to eat leftover picadillo is with steamed brown rice, black beans, and sour cream. *Serves 4; makes enough picadillo for 6*

To prepare the picadillo, put the raisins and orange juice in a small bowl and set aside.

Generously coat a large sauté pan with oil and heat the oil over medium-low heat for about 1 minute, just so you aren't adding onion to stone-cold oil. Add the onion, bay leaf (if you're using it), and chile, sprinkle with 1 teaspoon of the salt, and sauté, stirring often, for about 20 minutes, until the onion is very soft and beginning to turn to mush adding a splash of water to the pan from time to time to prevent the onion from sticking or browning. (The excessive cooking down of onion here is to bring flavor to a dish that is made with flavor-challenged meat.) Add the garlic and sauté, stirring so it doesn't brown, for 1 to 2 minutes, until fragrant. Add the tomato paste and cook for 1 minute to caramelize it. Add the turkey and sprinkle it with the cinnamon and the remaining 1 teaspoon salt. Cook for about 2 minutes, breaking up the meat with a spatula or wooden spoon as it cooks, until you have cooked off the pink color but not so long that the meat browns. Add the tomatoes and cook for a few minutes to reduce slightly. Add

recipe continues

FOR THE WALNUT CREMA

1 cup walnuts, soaked for at least 2 hours or blanched for 30 seconds in boiling water

1 tablespoon sugar

½ teaspoon kosher salt

FOR THE BOWLS

Poblano Rice (recipe follows) or 1 cup

Seeds from 1 pomegranate (about 1 cup; see sidebar, page 168)

Long-grain brown rice or quinoa, cooked (see page 30 or 42; about 3½ cups cooked grains)

enough stock to barely cover the meat. Bring the liquid to a simmer, reduce the heat to low, and cook for 1 hour, adding more stock to the pan when the pan is dry, until you've added all the stock. Add the raisins with the orange juice and cook for 5 minutes to cook off the juice. Turn off the heat and stir in the almonds. Taste and adjust the seasoning, adding more salt or spices if you're so inspired.

To prepare the walnut cream, drain the walnuts in a strainer and rub them between your hands or use a sink sprayer to remove any loose skins. (Leave any portion of the skins that doesn't come off easily.) Transfer the walnuts to a blender. Add the sugar, salt, and ½ cup water and puree.

To serve, spoon the rice into four wide bowls or onto four plates. Spoon ½ cup of picadillo on top of each serving of rice. Drizzle the walnut cream over the top, sprinkle with the pomegranate seeds, and serve. *Makes about 3½ cups*

Poblano Rice

1 poblano chile

1 cup long-grain brown rice, rinsed

1 teaspoon kosher salt

Heat a cast-iron skillet over high heat. Put the chile in the pan and cook until it's charred on all sides and has collapsed, about 10 minutes. Remove the chile from the heat and put it in a plastic bag. Close the bag and set it aside until the chile is cool enough to touch. Rub the bag against the pepper and the skins will stay in the bag; or use a clean dishtowel to remove and discard the charred skin. (Don't rinse the chile under water or you'll rinse away the char you just smoked up your kitchen to achieve.) Remove and discard the core and seeds and dice the chile.

Combine the rice, salt, diced poblano, and 2 cups water in a large straight-sided sauté pan and bring the water to a boil over high heat. Reduce the heat to low, cover, and simmer the rice for 20 to 30 minutes, until all the liquid has been absorbed and the rice is tender. Turn off the heat and let the rice rest, covered, for 10 minutes. Uncover and fluff gently with a fork.

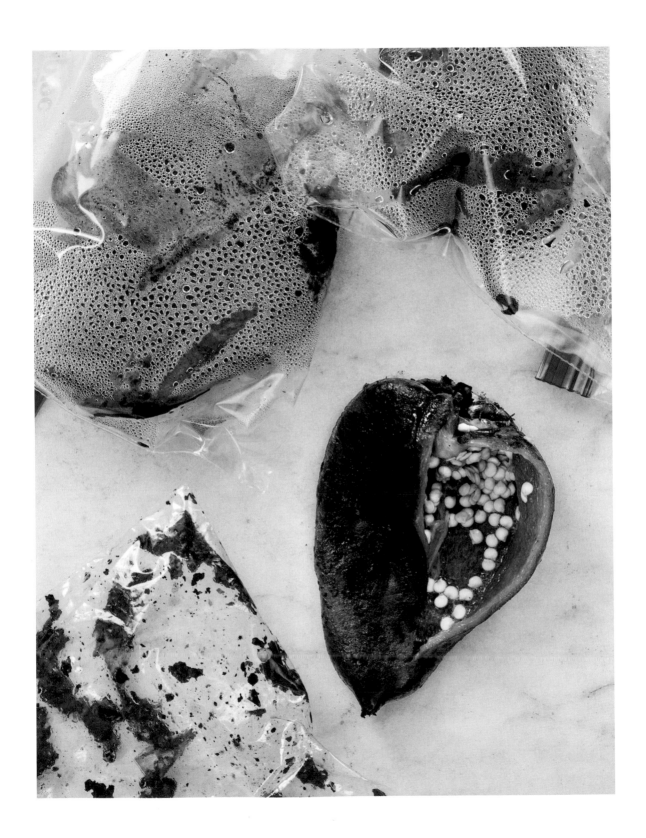

RED RICE PAD THAI
with Tofu and Shrimp

2 tablespoons tamarind
pulp

2 tablespoons fresh
lime juice

2 tablespoons soy sauce

2 tablespoons fish sauce

2 teaspoons light or dark
brown sugar

1 teaspoon kosher salt

Canola oil (or another
neutral-flavored oil)

8 ounces large (16 to 20
per pound) shrimp, peeled
and deveined

5 ounces firm tofu, drained
and cut into ½-inch cubes

4 eggs, lightly beaten

1 cup Thai red rice or
long-grain brown rice,
cooked (see page 42 or 36;
about 3 cups cooked rice)

2 garlic cloves, grated on a
Microplane or minced

3 cups bean sprouts

1 bunch scallions, white
and light green parts only,
thinly sliced on an angle

1 cup fresh basil (preferably
Thai basil)

1 cup fresh mint

1 cup roasted salted
peanuts (or cashews),
coarsely chopped

2 limes, halved, for garnish

Thai food and I have a complicated relationship. I absolutely love the flavors, but I rarely feel good after eating it. I started making this rice dish so I could eat pad thai and still walk among the living the next day. It has all the exotic contrasting sweet and sour flavors of pad thai without all the MSG and grease of so many restaurant versions.

I use Thai red rice here because of the reddish color of pad thai, but brown rice works, too. *Serves 4*

Dissolve the tamarind pulp in a small bowl with 3 tablespoons warm water, breaking up the pulp with a fork to help it dissolve. Stir in the lime juice, soy sauce, fish sauce, brown sugar, and salt.

Add enough oil to coat a large nonstick skillet (or a wok if you have one) and heat the oil over medium-high heat until it slides like water in the pan and is sizzling hot but not smoking, 2 to 3 minutes. Add the shrimp and tofu and sauté, with a spatula, until the shrimp are pink on both sides and the tofu is golden brown all over, about 4 minutes. Pour the eggs into the pan and tilt to coat the bottom of the pan and catch the tofu and shrimp in the egg "pancake." Working quickly so the eggs don't overcook, break up the eggs with the spatula, then slide the contents of the skillet onto a plate.

While the skillet is still hot, add enough oil to coat it and heat the oil for 20 or 30 seconds, until it's sizzling hot. Add the rice, and add the garlic on top of the rice (adding the garlic directly to the pan will cause it to burn instantly). Cook, stirring, for about 3 minutes to warm the rice through and cook the garlic. Return the eggs, shrimp, and tofu to the pan and add the bean sprouts, scallions, and tamarind mixture. Toss the ingredients together with the spatula and cook for about 2 minutes to heat through. Turn off the heat and stir in the basil and mint, leaving a few for garnish.

Divide the rice among four bowls and top with the peanuts and the remaining herbs. Serve the lime halves on the side for squeezing over the top.

MEZZE BOWL
with Pomegranate-Glazed Lamb Meatballs, Hummus, and Tzatziki

FOR THE MEATBALLS

2 pounds ground lamb (preferably American lamb)

1 teaspoon ground cumin

1 teaspoon ground coriander

1 teaspoon ground cinnamon

1 teaspoon ground allspice

½ teaspoon freshly ground black pepper

2 teaspoons kosher salt

¾ cup finely chopped Spanish yellow onion (about ½ small onion)

¾ cup finely chopped fresh parsley (about 1 bunch)

½ cup brown rice, cooked

1 egg, lightly beaten

3 garlic cloves, grated on a Microplane or minced

Olive oil

2 cups chicken stock, homemade (page 79) or sodium-free or low-sodium store-bought, or as needed

½ cup pomegranate molasses, plus more as needed

FOR THE BOWLS

Hummus (recipe follows)

3 cups Spiced Rice and Lentils, Pomegranate Tabbouleh, or steamed brown rice (see page 143, 168, or 36)

Tzatziki (recipe follows)

Handful of fresh flat-leaf parsley and mint

The less you work the meat, the lighter and more tender your meatballs will be.

I think I could convert any lamb hater with these meatballs. You have Emily Corliss to thank for them. Emily is a chef alum from Pizzeria Mozza who conspired with me on these recipes and she alone is responsible for the fact that these may be the most delicious lamb meatballs the world has ever known. We use cooked rice as a binder, which makes for extra-light, tender, and gluten-free meatballs. This recipe makes a lot of meatballs but they keep in the fridge for several days. You can even freeze the cooked meatballs—and who wouldn't want to come home hungry and find a lamb meatball waiting for them? The cooked meatballs are rolled in pomegranate molasses, which gives them a sweet-and-sour tang and takes them to the next level. You can find pomegranate molasses at Middle Eastern stores and specialty grocery stores. If you don't track it down, don't worry: the meatballs are so good without it, you'll wonder how there could even *be* a next level. *Makes 18 to 20 meatballs; serves 6*

To prepare the meatballs, put the lamb in a large bowl and add the rest of the ingredients except the oil, stock, and molasses. Gently knead the meat to distribute the ingredients throughout.

Scoop ¼ cup of the meat mixture and gently form the meat into an oblong. Put the balls on a plate or baking sheet and form the rest of the meatballs. Cover the meatballs and put them in the refrigerator to chill for at least 30 minutes and up to overnight. (Chilling the meatballs isn't crucial, but it does help prevent the balls from falling apart when they're cooked. It's also a handy make-ahead trick.)

Adjust the oven racks so one is in the middle position and preheat the oven to 325°F.

Coat a large straight-sided skillet with olive oil and heat the oil over high heat until it slides like water in the pan and is sizzling hot but not smoking. Add half the meatballs to the pan and cook for 3 to 4 minutes to sear all over, rolling them around so they cook evenly. Transfer the meatballs to a plate and

cook the second batch. Transfer the second batch to the plate.

Carefully, without burning yourself, use a bunched-up paper towel to wipe the fat and browned bits from the pan. Return the meatballs to the pan. Add enough stock to reach halfway up the side of the meatballs and put them in the oven to cook for 20 minutes. Remove the meatballs from the oven and let them rest in the cooking liquid for 10 minutes, or until you're ready to serve them.

To prepare the bowls, use the back of a spoon to smear a big swish of hummus on the bottom of four bowls. Pile a scoop of rice or tabbouleh on top.

Pour the pomegranate molasses into a medium bowl. Put a few meatballs in the molasses and roll them around to coat them. Take them out, put them on one of the waiting bowls, and roll the rest of the meatballs around in the molasses. Spoon the tzatziki next to the meatballs and use scissors to snip the parsley and mint so they fall directly onto the bowls.

recipe continues

Hummus

There are so many great packaged hummus brands available these days that you think it's not worth the time to make your own, until you do. First, it takes almost *no* time, so it doesn't have to be worth much. Second, to tell you how great homemade hummus is especially that made from homemade chickpeas, I'll quote my friend Dave Hermsen, who took one bite and said, "Hey, yo. This isn't regular ol' hummus. This shit is the bomb!" To make beet hummus, which admittedly is mostly for looks (the beet doesn't add a lot of flavor), add half a small roasted beet when you puree the hummus. *Makes about 2 cups*

1½ cups cooked chickpeas (page 104) or 1 (15-ounce) can chickpeas, drained and rinsed

¼ cup tahini (sesame seed paste)

¼ cup fresh lemon juice

2 garlic cloves

1 teaspoon kosher salt

Combine all the ingredients with 3 tablespoons water in a blender or food processor. Puree until the hummus is smooth; add more water if necessary to achieve a smooth consistency.

Tzatziki

Tzatziki is a Greek condiment of yogurt and cucumbers. The way I make it, with the cucumbers sliced instead of grated or minced, it's like a salad and condiment in one. Persian cucumbers are everything you want in a cucumber; they're sweet, crispy, seedless, and have thin skins, so you don't have to peel them. Japanese cukes are equally good, but not as easy to find. *Makes about 1½ cups*

1 cup plain Greek yogurt

2 garlic cloves, grated on a Microplane or minced

1 tablespoon fresh lemon juice

1 tablespoon chopped fresh dill

½ teaspoon kosher salt

2 Persian or Japanese cucumbers (or ½ peeled English cucumber), sliced ¼ inch thick

Stir the yogurt, garlic, lemon juice, dill, and salt together in a medium bowl. Fold in the cucumbers just before serving, to keep them nice and crunchy.

SUNDAY NIGHT DETOX BOWL
with Roasted Broccoli and Ponzu

1½ to 2 pounds broccoli (about 1 large head)

2 tablespoons canola oil (or another neutral-flavored oil)

1 teaspoon kosher salt

Ginger Scallion Rice (page 135), or 1 cup long-grain brown rice, cooked (see page 36; about 3½ cups cooked rice)

2 ripe avocados, halved, pitted, and peeled

1 lemon, quartered

Ponzu Sauce (recipe follows)

Broccoli flowers (optional)

Togarashi (or furikake or toasted black or white sesame seeds)

I do not have the digestive system to be a food writer. All the multicourse dinners, the food events, the recipe testing, the tasting. I know, not exactly a sob story. Still—in the words of a long-lost friend from Rome—eating this way makes my liver hurt. This bowl is what I eat when my liver hurts: a big bowl of brown rice piled with broccoli. Adding ponzu sauce and maybe, *maybe*, an avocado is as decadent as I want to go. The morning after eating this bowl I wake up and I can hear the faint sound of my renewed organ whispering, "*Grazie, Carolina. Grazie!*" Togarashi is a Japanese spice blend. You can use furikake (another Japanese seasoning, made of seaweed) or toasted sesame seeds instead. All of these can be found in the Asian section of upscale grocery stores, or in Asian grocery stores. *Serves 4*

Adjust the oven racks so none are near the oven floor; you will put the baking sheet on the oven floor. (If you have an oven that doesn't allow you to put a baking sheet on the floor, put one rack as close to it as possible.) Preheat the oven to 500°F.

Cut off and discard the tough stems of the broccoli and cut the broccoli into big tree-like segments. Put the trees on a baking sheet, toss with the oil and salt, and arrange them cut-side down in a single layer. Put the baking sheet on the oven floor or lowest rack and roast the broccoli for 10 to 12 minutes, until deep brown on both sides, turning the trees with tongs midway through the cooking time. Remove the broccoli from the oven.

(Alternatively, if you *really* want to make your liver happy, steam the broccoli until it is bright green and tender when pierced with a fork.)

Spoon the rice into four bowls. Put one avocado pitted-side up on each bowl. Nestle the broccoli and lemon wedges next to the avocado halves and drizzle the ponzu into the hole left by the avocado pits and over the broccoli and sprinkle with the broccoli flowers, if using. The broccoli flowers are just for looks—and absolutely optional. Sprinkle togarashi over the bowls and serve the rest of the ponzu sauce on the side.

recipe continues

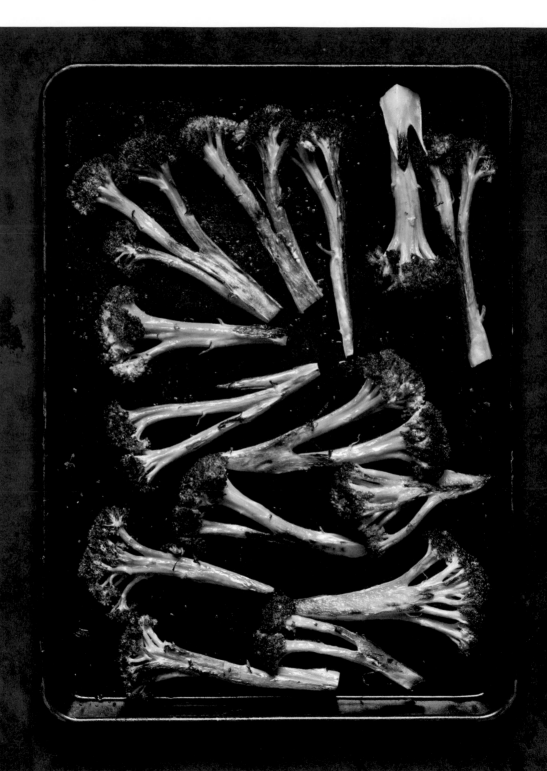

Ponzu Sauce

Ponzu sauce is a great "bomb shelter condiment." It takes about 2 minutes to make, out of ingredients you're very likely to have on hand. This sauce, a boiled egg, and a bowl of steamed brown rice and I'm happy.

Makes about 1¼ cups

¼ cup fresh lime juice

¼ cup fresh lemon juice

½ cup low-sodium soy sauce or tamari

2 tablespoons mirin (Japanese sweet rice wine; substitute dry sherry)

2 tablespoons rice vinegar

¼ teaspoon kosher salt

Stir all the ingredients together in a small bowl or glass measuring cup, or give them a shake in a clean jam jar with a lid. The sauce will keep, refrigerated, for up to a week.

Build Your Own Mexican Bowl

PROTEINS

Carne Asada

Baja BBQ Shrimp

Mole Chicken

Turkey Picadillo

Black Beans

GRAINS

Corn Rice or Quinoa

Mexican Restaurant Rice

Poblano Rice

Brazilian Rice

Plain rice or quinoa

VEGETABLES

Avocado

Cilantro

Chopped white onion

Shredded lettuce or green cabbage

Limes

Thinly sliced radishes

CONDIMENTS

Salsa

Mexican crema or sour cream

Cashew Crema

Queso fresco

Aji

Bottled Mexican
hot sauce

ULTIMATE BURRITO BOWL

FOR CARNE OR POLLO ASADA

1 bunch fresh cilantro

½ cup fresh lime juice

¾ cup beer (light or dark—doesn't matter)

1 white onion, cut into chunks to fit in the blender

3 garlic cloves

1 teaspoon kosher salt

1 red or green serrano or jalapeño, stemmed (optional)

1 to 1½ pounds skirt steak or skinless boneless chicken breasts or thighs

Freshly ground black pepper

Canola oil

1 lime, halved

Maldon, fleur de sel, or another flaky sea salt (optional; use it if you have it)

FOR THE BOWLS

Mexican Restaurant Rice (recipe follows) or Corn Rice or Quinoa (page 200) (or 1½ cups long-grain brown rice or quinoa, cooked (see page 36 or 42; about 3½ cups cooked grains)

3 cups cooked black beans (page 84), or 2 (15-ounce) cans, warmed in their liquid

Smoky Tomato Salsa (recipe follows; or your favorite store-bought salsa)

The burrito bowl is the "gateway" bowl for many health-conscious eaters. For the home cook, they're an easy, approachable way to turn all the deliciousness you'd find in a burrito into something that feels like more of a grown-up, sit-down meal. In this recipe, I give you a lot of options, from carne asada to vegan Chipotle Cashew Crema, so you can custom build the burrito bowl of your *sueños*. Because, in my opinion, like snowflakes, no two burrito bowls should be alike.

Skirt steak, used for the carne asada (which simply means "grilled meat"), is a very flavorful and juicy cut, and a lot less expensive than, say, rib-eye. Sear it over the hottest heat you can muster so the outside is charred and the inside stays juicy, slice it against the grain, and you and skirt steak will become fast friends. *Serves 4 to 6*

To prepare the carne asada, tear off the leafy portion of the cilantro bunches (grab the whole bunch at the neck and twist it off) and discard the long stems (or juice them). Throw the cilantro in a blender or food processor. Add the lime juice, beer, onion, garlic, kosher salt, and chile, if you're using it, and puree. Put the steak or chicken in a glass or ceramic baking dish or in a zip-top plastic bag and pour the marinade over it. (If you're making a combination, put them in two separate vessels because of the dangers of salmonella.) Turn the meat so the marinade coats all sides. Cover the bowl or close the bag and put it in the refrigerator to marinate the meat for 2 to 4 hours (any longer and the lime juice will begin to cook the meat). Remove the meat from the marinade. Scrape the marinade off the surface and season with the kosher salt and lots of pepper.

Brush a cast-iron skillet or grill pan with oil and heat over high heat until it is sizzling hot. (A drop of water will dance around when sprinkled onto it.) Lay the steak or chicken in the pan and sear without moving it until the meat is deep brown and caramelized, 3 to 4 minutes. (Moving the meat keeps it from browning, and that brown, caramelized flavor is what makes this steak special; otherwise, it's just a thin slab of gray meat.) For steak, turn and sear it to a deep brown on the second side, about 3 minutes for medium-rare, longer for medium or well-done meat. For chicken, reduce the heat to medium and cook for about 5 minutes, until the chicken is cooked through; the juices will run clear (not pink) when the chicken is pierced with a sharp knife and the chicken will register 165°F on an instant-read thermometer.

Transfer the steak or chicken to a cutting board and sprinkle with the lime juice and sea salt (if you have it). Let the meat rest for a few minutes, then thinly slice the steak against the grain. Slicing meat against the grain means your knife blade will be at an angle, not parallel to, the natural lines of the meat.

To serve, fill the bowls with the grain of your choice and spoon the beans to one side. Serve the steak, chicken, and condiments on the side for people to build their own ultimate burrito bowl.

OPTIONAL CONDIMENTS

Chipotle Cashew Crema
(recipe follows)

Mexican crema (or
sour cream thinned to a
drizzling consistency with
water or milk)

½ head green cabbage or
iceberg lettuce, cored and
thinly sliced

2 avocados, halved, pitted,
peeled, and sprinkled with
lime juice and salt

1 cup crumbled queso
fresco (or grated queso
cotija)

Finely chopped fresh
cilantro mixed with equal
parts finely chopped white
onion

Roasted salted pepitas or
cashews

Limes, halved

Chipotle Cashew Crema

Chipotle chiles are smoked jalapeño peppers. Chipotle chiles en adobo, which is what is called for here, come in a can; the "en adobo" refers to the marinade the peppers are packed in. Open up the can (which you can find these days at any ol' grocery store) and dump the entire contents into a blender or mini food processor. Swish out the can with a tablespoon or two of water and throw that water in the blender, too. Give it a whirl, and you now have the most delicious, spicy, smoky paste you've ever dreamed of. Put your precious paste into an old jam jar or other container and keep it in the fridge; it'll last for months. Spoon it into barbecue sauce, mayonnaise, marinades, chicken soup, black beans, chili, salsa, or sour cream. You'll never look at Sriracha the same way again. *Makes about 1 cup*

1 cup raw cashews, soaked for at least 1 hour and as long as overnight

1 teaspoon kosher salt

1 tablespoon agave syrup, or 2 tablespoons sugar

2 chipotle chiles en adobo

Drain the cashews, reserving 1 cup of the soaking liquid.

Put all the ingredients, including the reserved soaking liquid, in a blender and puree. The end.

Smoky Tomato Salsa

If there were one recipe in all of the world that I could pry out of someone, it would be the chipotle salsa recipe at Lotería Grill in Los Angeles. The owner, Jimmy Shaw, is a friend. And I've begged. But he still won't give it to me. I do my best to make a chipotle salsa as good as his. I think I come close, but I'm still working on Jimmy. *Makes about 3 cups*

1½ pounds Roma (plum) tomatoes

2 large Spanish yellow onions, sliced ½ to 1 inch thick

4 garlic cloves, unpeeled

2 chipotle chiles en adobo

2 teaspoons kosher salt

Heat a large cast-iron skillet or griddle over high heat until it is sizzling hot. Add the tomatoes, onion slices, and garlic, and cook, turning the vegetables so they cook evenly, until they are black in places and very soft, about 15 minutes. Have a plate nearby and transfer the veggies to the plate as they are done. Put the vegetables in a blender or food processor. Add the chipotle chiles and salt, and puree. The salsa will keep, refrigerated, for up to a week.

recipe continues

Mexican Restaurant Rice

At a certain type of Mexican restaurant in Southern California, those that specialize in combo platters covered with a blanket of melted orange cheese and a mountain of shredded iceberg, there is a rice that goes by the name of "Spanish rice," which I doubt has ever once been served in Spain. That rice is Southern California comfort food, and it has a special place in my heart. This rice is my version of that one. To make it vegan, cook the rice with vegetable stock or water instead of chicken stock. Use leftover rice for the Huevos Rancheros Bowl (page 83) or top with a fried egg, crema, and *queso cotija*. Perfection. This recipe assumes a sodium-free stock; if your stock has any sodium in it at all, cut the salt in this recipe in half. *Makes about 6 cups*

Canola oil (or another neutral-flavored oil)

1 medium Spanish yellow onion, finely chopped

2 teaspoons kosher salt

2 cups long-grain brown rice, rinsed

6 garlic cloves, grated on a Microplane or minced

3½ cups chicken stock, homemade (page 79), sodium-free or low-sodium store-bought, or water

¼ cup Smoky Tomato Salsa (page 193; or another pureed salsa, or pureed tomatoes)

1 lime, halved

Add enough oil to generously coat a large straight-sided sauté pan and heat over medium heat until the oil is hot and slides like water in the pan but isn't smoking. Add the onion and salt and cook, stirring often, until it is soft and translucent, about 6 minutes. Add the rice and cook, stirring often, until it is golden brown and toasty smelling, about 4 minutes. Add the garlic and cook for about 1 minute, until it is fragrant; don't let it brown. Add the stock and salsa and bring the liquid to a simmer. Cover the pot, reduce the heat to low, and gently simmer the rice until the liquid is absorbed, about 40 minutes. Turn off the heat and let the rice rest for 10 minutes. Uncover, squeeze the lime juice over the rice, and fluff gently with a fork.

KOREAN SHORT RIBS
with Kimchi Rice

1 cup low-sodium soy sauce or tamari

1 cup packed light or dark brown sugar

1 ripe Asian pear (or another pear), halved, cored, and cut into chunks to fit in the blender

½ Spanish yellow onion, cut into chunks to fit in the blender

1 (2-inch) piece fresh ginger, peeled and cut into a few pieces

4 garlic cloves

½ teaspoon red pepper flakes (optional)

2 pounds Korean-cut short ribs (ask your butcher for flanken-cut ribs, sliced ⅓ inch thick)

Kosher salt and freshly ground black pepper

Canola oil (or another neutral-flavored oil)

Toasted white sesame seeds, for sprinkling

4 to 6 scallions, white and light green parts, thinly sliced

Kimchi Rice (recipe follows)

Fresh lettuce leaves, for serving (optional)

1 cup sugar snap peas, thinly sliced, for serving (optional)

There is only one way to eat Korean short ribs, and that is with your hands.

When I was working on a meat encyclopedia cum cookbook with the celebrity butcher Pat LaFrieda, I don't think I'd ever seen him more excited than when he talked about discovering Korean-cut short ribs for the first time. Korean-cut short ribs are cut very thin and marinated before being thrown on a hot grill, where they cook in minutes. Pat, being a fourth-generation butcher and all-around meat geek, knows more or less everything there is to know about meat. Except, as it turned out, this one thing. "In all my life as a butcher," he said, "I had never seen this. Just by cutting the meat differently, you took something that normally takes hours to cook and you were able to cook it in minutes." I recommend you try this very tasty magic trick at home.

For this recipe, you have to think ahead because the secret to their tenderness is to get the ribs in the marinade the day before you're going to cook them; the acidity in the fruit that's in the marinade tenderizes the meat. The Kimchi Rice I serve them with also requires that you start ahead. I designed it this way. *Serves 4*

Combine the soy sauce, brown sugar, pear, onion, ginger, garlic, and red pepper flakes (if you're using them) in a blender and puree. Put the short ribs in a shallow glass or ceramic baking dish or a large zip-top plastic bag. Add the marinade and turn the ribs to coat them on both sides. Cover the dish with plastic wrap or zip the bag closed and put the ribs in the refrigerator to tenderize overnight.

When you're ready to cook the ribs, remove them from the refrigerator. Line a baking sheet with paper towels. Take the ribs out of the marinade and put them on the paper towels to drain the excess marinade.

Heat a cast-iron grill pan over high heat or preheat an outdoor grill to very hot and brush the pan or grill gates with oil. Season the ribs lightly with salt and pepper on both sides. Put the ribs in the pan or on the grill and cook until they have dark grill marks and are charred in places, 1½ to 2 minutes per side. (You will need to cook the ribs in batches.) Transfer the ribs to a cutting board.

Cut the ribs between the bones into easy-to-hold segments or serve with scissors for people to cut their own. Shower the sesame seeds and scallions on top and serve the ribs with the rice, lettuce and sugar snap peas, if you're using them.

Kimchi Rice

Kimchi is Korean fermented cabbage. It has a funky, sour flavor that I would describe as an acquired taste—and I haven't acquired it. But in recent years, foodies (and in particular, health foodies) *have* acquired that taste and have become obsessed with kimchi, both eating and making it. The cabbage in this rice is fermented for just 8 hours, so it doesn't have the funky flavor of authentic kimchi. Whether you consider that a good thing or not is totally a matter of taste. For me, it's a great thing. Top leftover kimchi rice with a fried egg and a scribble of Sriracha.

Makes about 4 cups

½ head napa or green cabbage, cored and cut into 1-inch slices

3 tablespoons kosher salt

1 cup long-grain brown rice, cooked (see page 36; about 3½ cups cooked rice)

¼ cup rice vinegar

2 tablespoons Sriracha

3 scallions, trimmed and thinly sliced into rings (white and light green parts)

1 carrot, cut into ¼-inch cubes

2 tablespoons sugar

1 (1-inch) piece fresh ginger, peeled and grated on a Microplane or minced (about 1 teaspoon)

2 garlic cloves, grated on a Microplane or minced

Put the cabbage in a big bowl and toss with the salt. Transfer the cabbage to a colander and set the colander in a bowl. Set aside at room temperature for at least 8 hours and as long as overnight.

Transfer the cabbage to a large bowl and fill the bowl with water. Use your hands to agitate the cabbage and release as much salt as possible. Lift the cabbage out of the water and return it to the colander (don't just dump the contents of the bowl into the colander, as you'd be pouring the salty water back over the cabbage and you're trying to get the salt *out* of the cabbage). Rinse out the bowl, return the cabbage to the bowl, and repeat: fill the bowl with water and agitate the cabbage, and lift it out of the water and back into the colander. Let the cabbage drain completely. Transfer it to a cutting board and run your knife through it two or three times to chop it into bite-size pieces.

Put the cabbage back in the bowl. Add the rest of the ingredients and toss to combine. Serve warm.

BAJA BBQ SHRIMP BOWL
with Corn Rice

FOR THE SHRIMP

Canola oil (or another neutral-flavored oil)

3 garlic cloves, smashed with the side of a knife

1 pound large shrimp (16 to 20 per pound), peeled and deveined

1 teaspoon kosher salt

1 tablespoon pureed chipotle chile en adobo

1 tablespoon tomato paste (from a tube), or 2 tablespoons regular tomato paste

1 tablespoon low-sodium soy sauce or tamari

1 tablespoon dark brown sugar

1 lime, halved

FOR THE BOWLS

Corn Rice or Quinoa (recipe follows; Brazilian Rice, Poblano Rice, or plain steamed brown rice or quinoa (see page 207, 180, 36, or 42; 3 to 4 cups cooked grains)

3 cups cooked black beans (page 84), or 2 (15-ounce) cans, warmed in their canning liquid

½ head green cabbage (or iceberg lettuce), cored and thinly sliced

Mexican crema (or sour cream thinned to a drizzling consistency with water or milk; or Chipotle Cashew Crema, page 193)

2 limes, halved

In the name of "write what you know," one of the first stories I did for *Saveur* was about fish tacos. During summer vacations when I was in high school, my friends and I used to drive from San Diego, where I grew up, south into Mexico, where we would stay at a friend's parents' house in one of the beach towns near Ensenada. For days on end, we would lather our bodies in coconut oil and fry under the hot summer sun, indulge in the underage consumption of mini Corona beers, and eat tempura-battered fish and shrimp tacos sold from roadside stands. In researching the story, I discovered that Baja-style fish tacos are the invention of Japanese fishermen living in Ensenada, which allows me to justify putting soy sauce in these shrimp and still use the word "Baja" to describe them.

Don't tell any of my food snob friends, but I keep a pound of frozen shrimp in the freezer at all times. Since I am never without a can of chipotle chiles (which are available in most supermarkets), this bowl is always within reach. It's also gluten-free. *¡Que suerte! Serves 4*

To prepare the shrimp, add enough oil to a large skillet to coat it generously and add the garlic. Heat the garlic and oil together over medium-high heat until the oil is hot and slides like water in the pan but is not smoking. Add the shrimp, season with the salt, and cook until they are pink and opaque on both sides about 5 minutes. Reduce the heat to low and move the shrimp to one side of the pan.

Add the chipotle puree, tomato paste, soy sauce, and brown sugar and cook for 1 to 2 minutes to meld the flavors. Turn off the heat, squeeze the lime over the shrimp, and toss again.

To assemble the bowls, spoon the grains into four bowls and spoon the beans on top. Pile on the shrimp and cabbage. Drizzle crema over everything and serve each bowl with a lime half.

recipe continues

Corn Rice or Quinoa

I learned to make stock from corn cobs when I did an internship at Chez Panisse, the birthplace of the American farm-to-table movement, in Berkeley. Every morning, the chefs and interns would sit around a table while the chef planned the day's menu and we did any prep that could be done sitting down, which, because it was late summer, meant shucking corn. One day, the chefs decided to turn the corn into soup, and my job would be to make the corn stock. Thankfully one of the chefs walked me through the process, which went like this: Put the shucked corn cobs in a big stockpot, add enough water to cover the cobs, and simmer for about an hour. The resulting soup tasted like corn to the tenth degree, and the same, I've discovered, goes for rice and quinoa cooked in corn stock. Since then, I've rarely let a raw corn cob go into the trash without first boiling out all it has to give.

Warning: I tried making this with ordinary supermarket corn, as opposed to farmers' market or Chino Ranch corn, and the grains had almost no corn flavor. If you don't want to go to a farmers' market, or corn isn't in season, don't waste your time boiling flavorless cobs. Just make another grain instead. The addition of grated cotija cheese and Chipotle Cashew Crema turns corn rice into a rich and delicious side dish.

Makes about 4 cups

3 ears corn, shucked, kernels cut from the cobs, and cobs reserved

1 cup long-grain brown rice or quinoa, rinsed

2 teaspoons kosher salt

Olive oil

½ teaspoon sugar (optional)

3 or 4 scallions, white and light green parts only, thinly sliced (optional)

Put the corn cobs in a tall stockpot with an insert, if you have one, or else in any large pot and add 7 cups water. Bring the water to a boil over high heat. Reduce the heat to maintain a simmer and cook the cobs for 45 minutes to 1 hour, until the liquid has reduced by half and the stock is corn colored and flavorful. Lift out the insert or strain the stock into a large glass measuring cup or a large bowl and discard the solids.

Measure out 3½ cups of the corn stock. (Save any leftover for the next time you cook grains; if you don't have enough, supplement water.) Pour the stock into a large saucepan. Add the rice or quinoa and 1 teaspoon of the salt and bring the stock to a boil over high heat. Reduce the heat so the liquid is barely simmering, put the lid on the pan, and cook until the liquid has been absorbed, about 20 minutes for quinoa, 20 to 30 minutes for rice. Turn off the heat and let the grains rest, covered, for 10 minutes. Uncover and fluff gently with a fork.

While the grains are cooking, pour enough oil to coat a large skillet and heat the oil over high heat until it is searing hot (it will slide like water in the pan) but not smoking, 2 to 3 minutes; the corn should sizzle when it touches the pan. Add the corn kernels, sprinkle with the sugar (if you are using it) and the remaining 1 teaspoon salt, and cook, stirring and scraping up the corn that wants to stick to the pan with a metal spatula until the corn is caramelized and begins to snap, crackle, and pop, 4 to 6 minutes. Turn off the heat. Add the rice or quinoa and fold the grains and corn together for about 1 minute to warm the grains. Fold in the scallions and serve.

INDIAN CAULIFLOWER AND CHICKPEA CURRY
with Savory Yogurt and Millet

Canola oil (or another neutral-flavored oil)

1 red onion, halved and each half cut into 6 or 8 wedges

1 tablespoon kosher salt

1 big head of cauliflower, cored and cut into small florets

1 (15-ounce) can crushed tomatoes

1½ cups cooked chickpeas (page 104), or 1 (15-ounce) can chickpeas, drained and rinsed

2 cups vegetable stock or chicken stock, homemade (page 79) or sodium-free or low-sodium store-bought as needed

¼ cup curry powder

1 tablespoon garam masala (or curry powder)

1 tablespoon kosher salt

1½ teaspoons cayenne pepper

¾ cup plain Greek yogurt

1 cup loosely packed fresh cilantro leaves

Savory Yogurt (recipe follows)

1 cup millet, cooked (see page 40; 3 to 4 cups cooked millet)

Curry refers to any number of spice blends in India. Garam masala, one of the two curry powders called for in this recipe, is less known than yellow curry; it's an unusual, sweet-and-spicy blend that includes cumin, coriander, cardamom, cinnamon, and cloves, among other spices. If you can't find it, use whatever curry powder you do find. I serve this on millet because millet is a staple grain in India, but steamed rice or quinoa would be equally good here. All are gluten-free. This is a vegetarian dish; the sauce is made with yogurt so it's not vegan. I suppose one could try using coconut yogurt, but I'll leave that experiment to you. It makes a big portion because I made the recipe to call for one of everything: one onion, one head of cauliflower, one can of chickpeas, and one can of tomatoes. Plus, I'd rather eat leftovers than takeout. *Serves 6*

Pour enough oil to cover the surface of a large pot or Dutch oven heat the oil over medium-high heat for about 1 minute, just to warm it enough so that you aren't adding onion to cold oil. Add the onion, sprinkle it with 1 teaspoon of the salt, and cook, stirring often so it doesn't brown, for about 10 minutes, until the onion is tender and translucent. Add the cauliflower, sprinkle with 1 teaspoon of the remaining salt, and sauté another for 5 minutes to soften it slightly. Add the tomatoes, chickpeas, stock, curry powder, garam masala, cayenne, and the remaining 1 teaspoon of salt, simmer for 20 minutes, until the sauce has reduced and the cauliflower is tender but not mushy. Turn off the heat and fold in the ¾ cup of yogurt.

Smear a big swath of the Savory Yogurt on the bottom of each bowl. Spoon the millet and the curry on top, side by side. Sprinkle with the fresh cilantro and serve the remaining Savory Yogurt on the side.

Savory Yogurt

Stir these five ingredients together and meet your new favorite, healthy, and delicious condiment and friend to just about any grain bowl (that isn't Mexican). *Makes about 1 cup*

1 cup plain Greek yogurt

Juice of ½ lemon

2 peeled garlic cloves, grated on a Microplane or minced

1 tablespoon extra-virgin olive oil

½ teaspoon kosher salt

Stir all the ingredients together. End of story. The sauce will keep, refrigerated, for up to 5 days.

SORGHUM RISOTTO PRIMAVERA
with Bacon and Burrata

2 teaspoons kosher salt, plus more to taste

¾ cup sorghum, soaked for at least 1 hour and as long as overnight

¼ cup short- or long-grain brown rice, rinsed

4 slices thick-cut bacon

½ large Spanish yellow onion, finely chopped

½ cup dry white wine

4 cups chicken stock (preferably homemade, page 79; or sodium-free or low-sodium store-bought) or as needed

½ cup peas (preferably fresh shelled peas)

½ cup grated Parmesan cheese, plus more for sprinkling or grating

1 (8-ounce) ball burrata cheese

Small handful of fresh chives

This risotto is made with a combination of rice and sorghum, which has a mild flavor and chewy texture. Burrata is cream-filled mozzarella from Puglia, the "heel" of the boot that is Italy. When you cut open a ball of burrata, the rich cream spills out, like the cheese version of a Cadbury egg. Look for DiStefano burrata (available at Italian import stores and Whole Foods), which is made by Mimmo Bruno, a Pugliese cheese maker in Los Angeles, using cream from Parma left over from making Parmesan cheese. So it's Italian cream, but made fresh every day. The best of all worlds. This risotto is gluten-free. *Serves 4*

Bring 3 cups water to a boil in a small saucepan over high heat. Add 1 teaspoon of the salt, the sorghum, and the rice. Reduce the heat to maintain a simmer and cook for 35 minutes to partially cook the grains. Drain the grains or lift them out of the water with a strainer.

While the grains are cooking, cook the bacon in a large skillet over medium heat until the fat has rendered and the bacon is brown but not crispy, 5 to 10 minutes (the time varies depending on the thickness of the bacon). Transfer the bacon to a bed of paper towels to cool; thinly slice crosswise.

Add the onion to the pan with the bacon fat and sprinkle with the remaining 1 teaspoon salt. Sauté the onion, stirring often so it doesn't brown, until it is soft and translucent, 6 to 8 minutes. Add the sorghum and rice and the wine and cook for a minute or two until the grains have

drunk the wine. Add 1 cup of stock and cook, stirring often, until the grains have absorbed the liquid. Continue in this way, adding the stock 1 cup at a time, and allowing the grains to absorb the stock each time before adding more, until the risotto is creamy and the sorghum is tender, about 45 minutes. Add the peas and ½ cup of the remaining stock and cook until the peas are tender and not starchy, about 5 minutes. Turn off the heat and stir in the Parmesan and bacon. Stir in more stock or water if the cheese made the risotto too thick; you want it to be loose enough to spread out when you dish it into a flat bowl.

Spoon the risotto into four bowls. Dollop a quarter of the burrata onto each bowl. Use scissors to snip chives over each serving, and serve with Parmesan on the table for sprinkling or grating.

BRAZILIAN BOWL
with Quick-Cooked Collard Greens and Ají

FOR THE SQUASH

2 acorn squash or 3 to 4 medium Delicata squash, halved lengthwise, seeded, and sliced into ½-inch half-moons

2 tablespoons olive oil

1 teaspoon kosher salt

1 teaspoon smoked paprika (optional; or red pepper flakes)

FOR THE GREENS

1 bunch collard greens

Olive oil

2 garlic cloves, grated on a Microplane or minced

1 teaspoon kosher salt

FOR THE BOWLS

Brazilian Rice (recipe follows; or 1 cup brown rice, cooked (see page 36; about 3½ cups cooked rice)

1½ to 2 cups cooked black beans (see page 84) or 1 (15-ounce) can, warmed in their canning liquid

Ají (recipe follows) or the hot sauce of your choice

1 jalapeño, very thinly sliced

In Los Angeles, there's a place called Farmers Market at Third and Fairfax, which isn't a farmers' market at all, but an open air plaza with open seating and a bunch of food stalls—some dating back to the 1930s. The stalls originated as stands to provide coffee and cooked food to the farmers who came there to sell fruit, mostly citrus. There are many great places to eat at the Farmers Market, but the one with a wraparound line is the Brazilian joint that serves black beans, rice, garlicky shredded greens, butternut squash, plantains, beef stroganoff (go figure!), and grilled meats of every kind, which the handsome young Brazilian men who work there carve off skewers as tall as I am. This recipe is the bowl version of what my plate looks like after I pass through that line. I sometimes get a single tiny link of linguiça sausage, but more often than not, it's all rice, beans, and veg for me.

Collard greens, a dark green leafy vegetable, have big, smooth leaves, like green elephant ears. In the United States, they're popular in Southern cuisine, where they're cooked for so long and with so much pork fat that they hardly qualify as a vegetable. In this recipe, they're prepared in the traditional Brazilian way: shredded and cooked with garlic and olive oil for just a minute, to take off the raw edge. Because they're so quick to prepare, and so healthy, I cook these greens often for breakfast: leftover grain, these greens, a fried egg, and hot sauce. You're welcome.

This bowl is g-free and vegan. Unless, that is, you decide to sneak some grilled or pan-fried linguiça sausage slices into the mix. *Serves 4*

To prepare the squash, adjust the oven racks so none is near the oven floor; you are going to put the baking sheet on the oven floor. (If you have an oven that doesn't allow you to put a baking sheet on the floor, put a second rack as close to the floor as possible.) Preheat the oven to 500°F.

Toss the squash slices on a baking sheet with the oil, salt, and paprika or pepper flakes, if you're using them, and lay them flat in a single layer. Bake the squash on the oven floor or lowest rack until the sides touching the pan are deep brown, 5 to 6 minutes. Remove the baking sheet

from the oven and turn each half-moon with tongs. Return the squash to the oven to roast until the second side is deep brown, 5 to 6 minutes.

To prepare the greens, stack three or four collard leaves at a time and roll them lengthwise into a tight log. Cut across the log to thinly slice the leaves, stopping when you get to the stems, and discard the stems.

Pour enough oil to coat a large skillet and heat the oil over high heat for about 2 minutes, until it is searing hot and slides like water in the pan but is not smoking. Add the garlic and greens, season with the salt and cook, folding the greens with tongs, for 1 to 2 minutes, until they are bright, emerald green.

Spoon the rice and beans in the bowls. Lift the greens out of the skillet and onto the bowls and lay the squash on top. Drizzle each bowl with ají and scatter the jalapeño slices. Put on your favorite bossa nova mix, and eat.

Brazilian Rice

My Brazilian friend Eduardo introduced me to his mother's recipe for cooking white rice in chicken stock, which is so unbelievably delicious, it belies its simplicity. I adopted their recipe, but, naturally, I make mine with brown rice. I love the rice plain, straight from the pot, or I make a simple lunch of just rice, black beans, and ají (recipe follows) or pickled jalapeños. It's the ultimate comfort food, even if you're not Brazilian. This recipe assumes you are using sodium-free stock. If your stock has any sodium in it at all, cut the salt in half. *Makes about 3 cups*

Olive oil

½ medium Spanish yellow onion, finely chopped

1 teaspoon kosher salt

3 garlic cloves, grated on a Microplane or minced

1 cup long-grain brown or white rice, rinsed

4 cups chicken stock, homemade (page 79) or sodium-free or low-sodium store-bought

Liberally coat a medium saucepan with oil and heat the oil over medium heat for about 1 minute, just to warm it a bit. Add the onion, sprinkle with the salt, and sauté until tender and translucent, 6 to 8 minutes, stirring often so it doesn't brown. Add the garlic and cook, stirring continuously so the garlic doesn't brown, for 1 minute. Add the rice and cook, stirring continuously, for 1 to 2 minutes, until it is slightly pearlescent and begins to smell like rice. Add the stock plus 1 cup water and let it come to a simmer. Reduce the heat to medium-low and simmer uncovered and without stirring, until the rice has absorbed the stock and is tender, about 1 hour. Turn off the heat and let the rice rest for 10 minutes in the pan. Fluff the rice with a fork and serve.

recipe continues

Contrary to widespread belief, those little chips of chewy brown garlic are not what we're going for when we sauté garlic. Garlic cooked this way is bitter. If you let the garlic get that far, clean out the pan and start over.

Ají

Ají is a spicy salsa, made from raw chiles, onion, and cilantro, from South America. This recipe (a version of it anyway) is my takeaway from a book I wrote with the R&B singer Kelis. It's a total blast of bright, spicy green flavor. Spoon it on black beans, Corn Quinoa, or anything else with a south-of-the-border vibe. *Makes about 1 cup*

1 bunch fresh cilantro

2 tablespoons white wine vinegar

2 tablespoons fresh lime juice

1 bunch scallions, white and light green parts only, halved

½ large Spanish yellow onion, cut into chunks

2 serrano chiles, stemmed and seeded

4 garlic cloves

1 teaspoon kosher salt

Tear off the leafy portion of the cilantro bunches (grab the whole bunch at the neck and twist it off) and discard the long stems. Throw the cilantro in a blender. Add 2 tablespoons water and the rest of the ingredients and blast the blender until the ingredients are pureed, stopping to scrape down the sides of the blender jar once or twice in the process. Refrigerate in a covered container for up to a week.

DESSERT BOWLS

There are two types of people in the world: those who are indifferent to dessert, and those who cannot even begin to imagine being indifferent to dessert. I'm definitely in the second category. But even though I like dessert, I try not to eat most of what dessert is made of—namely, sugar and white flour. So I make some concessions. These desserts are made using whole grains and no flour. But they're also made with all the things that make dessert delicious: sugar (I use as little as I can get away with without compromising the dessert) and chocolate, cream and butter and eggs. So if you're looking for date-sweetened pastries with the texture of a Duraflame log, don't look here. Because if I'm going to eat dessert, I want it to be extraordinary. A treat. A little something to indulge in once in a while, and to love.

COCONUT BLACK AND WILD RICE PUDDING with Mangoes and Macadamia Nuts 212

MIXED BERRY CRISP with Whole-Grain Crisp Topping 215

SOURMASH APPLE CRISP with Whole-Grain Crisp Topping 217

FLOURLESS CHOCOLATE TEFF CAKE 218

QUINOA INDIAN PUDDING 222

DECONSTRUCTED ITALIAN EASTER PIE with Wheat Berries and Honey 224

WHOLE-GRAIN WHITE CHOCOLATE COMPOST 225

GOAT'S MILK RICE PUDDING with Cinnamon and Raisins 227

DARK CHOCOLATE FARRO GOOP with Toasted Walnuts and Steamed Cream 228

TOASTED MILLET FROZEN CUSTARD with Pan-Seared Fruit 230

COCONUT BLACK AND WILD RICE PUDDING
with Mangoes and Macadamia Nuts

½ cup wild rice, rinsed

¾ teaspoon kosher salt

½ cup black rice, rinsed

2 (15-ounce) cans coconut milk, shaken

½ cup plus 2 tablespoons raw or granulated sugar

1 ripe medium mango, peeled, pitted, and thinly sliced

½ cup roasted salted macadamia nuts or peanuts, finely chopped

Long before I ever soaked a chia seed or toasted a grain of millet, I made a version of the classic Thai dessert, coconut sticky rice. Even though I was a grain novice, I knew enough to know that black rice was a whole, unprocessed (healthy!) grain, and that coconut milk didn't have the negative effects on me and my digestion that cow's milk did, so I happily welcomed this harmless dessert into my life. This version combines black and wild rice just to mix things up in the texture department, and to add another layer of flavor. I've never met anyone who didn't love it. *Serves 4 to 6*

Combine the wild rice, salt, and 2 cups water in a medium saucepan and bring the water to a boil over high heat. Reduce the heat to maintain a simmer, cover, and cook for 15 minutes. Add the black rice and cook until the water has been absorbed, about 20 minutes more. Stir in the coconut milk and sugar and bring the milk to a boil over high heat. Reduce the heat to medium and simmer, uncovered, for about 20 minutes, stirring occasionally, until the pudding is thick with very little liquid remaining. Turn off the heat and let the rice rest for 10 minutes to thicken up and cool slightly. The rice is delicious warm or chilled. To chill, let the rice cool to room temperature, then transfer to the refrigerator. The rice will keep, refrigerated, for up to a week, but it will stiffen up like a block of butter. To bring it back to life, heat it over low heat with water or coconut milk until it's a lovely, loose consistency.

To serve, spoon the rice into four to six bowls. Lay the sliced mango over the top and shower with the nuts.

MIXED BERRY CRISP
with Whole-Grain Crisp Topping

3 (10- to 12-ounce) bags frozen small berries (raspberries, blackberries, blueberries, or boysenberries), or 7 cups fresh berries

¼ cup all-purpose, whole wheat, or brown rice flour

¼ cup plus 2 tablespoons raw or granulated sugar

1 tablespoon fresh lemon juice

Uncooked Whole-Grain Crisp Topping (recipe follows)

Yogurt Cream (page 72) or vanilla ice cream or whipped cream, for serving

Fruit crisp is the most obvious, organically whole-grain dessert there is, because the topping is traditionally made from rolled oats, and the filling consists of fruit and as much or as little sugar as you want to add to it. Crisps are also very forgiving.

If I were a die-hard seasonally inspired cook, I would tell you that this was strictly a summer crisp. But truth be told, I make it just as often in the winter, because I always have bags of fresh berries in the freezer just for this purpose. Whether you make this crisp with fresh or frozen fruit, it's the easiest dessert you'll ever put together because berries don't require any peeling, slicing, or dicing. Just dump and bake. *Serves 6 or more*

Adjust the oven racks so one is in the middle position and preheat the oven to 350°F.

Put the berries, flour, sugar, and lemon juice in a bowl and stir to combine. Dump the berries out into a large ovenproof skillet or a deep ceramic pie or casserole dish. Crumble the crisp topping over the fruit, leaving the fruit around the edges visible. Put the dish on a baking sheet to catch any juices that might bubble over and bake for about 50 minutes, until the fruit is bubbling around the edges and the topping is golden brown and crisp. Remove the crisp from the oven and let it cool for 10 minutes. Spoon it into bowls and serve with the cream of your choice.

recipe continues

Whole-Grain Crisp Topping

Years ago, when I was just starting out as a writer, I got a summer job baking fruit pies, cobblers, crisps, and cookies for the "One Percent" clientele who shopped at Loaves & Fishes, a legendarily expensive Hamptons gourmet food emporium. In addition to making 60 pies a day (with everything from scratch, of course), I made big portions of crisp topping, which we would freeze and use to put together fruit crisps at a moment's notice. Today, I do the same at home. Buckwheat is the latest addition to my ever-evolving crisp topping recipe. It adds such an appealing crunch that you almost forget about the fact that it's also good for you. To make it gluten-free, use brown rice flour, which results in a slightly grainier but still buttery and irresistible topping.

Bake this topping on the Sourmash Apple Crisp (page 217) or Mixed Berry Crisp (page 215). Or bake it on its own and sprinkle the crispy crumbles over Pan-Seared Fruit (page 233) or yogurt. *Makes about 2 cups, or enough for 1 fruit crisp*

¾ cup all-purpose, whole wheat, or brown rice flour

½ cup plus 2 tablespoons rolled oats (or any rolled cereal)

¼ cup plus 2 tablespoons packed light or dark brown sugar

¼ cup buckwheat

¼ teaspoon kosher salt

6 tablespoons (¾ stick) cold unsalted butter, cut into cubes

Adjust the oven racks so one is in the middle position and preheat the oven to 300°F.

Combine the flour, oats, brown sugar, buckwheat, and salt in a medium bowl. Add the butter and use your fingertips to work the butter in with the dry ingredients until no flour is visible and the mixture forms clumps. Use as a topping in the crisp recipe of your choice, or bake it on its own. If you're saving it for later, refrigerate the topping for up to a week in a covered container, or freeze for up to several months.

To bake the crisp topping on its own, spread it out on a baking sheet in a single layer, bringing any stray pieces into the main event; stray bits will burn before the rest is done. Bake for 15 to 20 minutes, until golden brown and crispy, stirring once or twice in the process so the topping browns and crisps up evenly. Remove the topping from the oven. If you're storing the topping to use later, let it cool, then store at room temperature in a covered container.

SOURMASH APPLE CRISP
with Whole-Grain Crisp Topping

3 pounds tart baking apples (such as Northern Spy, Pink Lady, Granny Smith, Honeycrisp, Braeburn, Cortland, or Pippin), peeled, cored, and cut into ¾-inch wedges

½ cup sugar

2 tablespoons Jack Daniel's (or another whiskey; optional)

1 tablespoon whole wheat, all-purpose, or rice flour

1 tablespoon fresh lemon juice

½ teaspoon ground cinnamon

Uncooked Whole-Grain Crisp Topping (page 216)

Vanilla ice cream, whipped cream, or Yogurt Cream (page 72), for serving

Before I got a job selling apples at the farmers' market in New York City, I thought I lived in a red-or-green-apple world. But the farm I worked for, Locust Grove, grew and sold twenty-seven varieties of what the farmer I worked for, Chip Kent, referred to as "antique apples." Antique apples are those grown from trees that were planted long before our priorities moved from how the apples *taste* to how the apples *look*, how long they last in cold storage, or how well they travel. The apples, crisp and juicy beyond any apple I'd eaten before, had names like Winter Banana, Black Twig, and Honeycrisp, and were irregularly sized, oddly shaped, lumpy and bumpy; Golden Russets even had a rough exterior like a potato. Helping customers choose from the immense variety was my favorite part of the job. When it came to pie apples, our favorite saying at the stand was, "Northern Spy for apple pie!" Northern Spies, like any good pie apple, hold their shape when they're baked, so you end up with yummy baked apples, not apple *sauce* under your crust. Use whatever variety of pie apples (listed in the recipe to the left) you can find, or better yet, use a mix.

In this recipe, the apples are cooked with Jack Daniel's, and once you try it you're going to think that every baked apple dessert should call for Jack Daniel's. You don't know you're tasting booze exactly, you just know you're eating a yummy, caramel-ly, apple-y dessert, and that you want more. *Serves 6 or more*

Adjust oven rack so one is in the middle position and preheat oven to 300°F.

Combine the apples, sugar, Jack Daniel's (if you're using it), flour, lemon juice, and cinnamon in a medium baking dish, pie pan, or skillet. Spread the crisp topping over it, leaving the fruit visible around the edges. Put the dish on a baking sheet to catch any juices that might bubble over and bake for about 45 minutes, until the fruit starts to bubble around the edges. Remove the crisp from the oven and let it cool for 10 minutes, then spoon it into bowls and serve with the cream of your choice.

FLOURLESS CHOCOLATE TEFF CAKE

15 ounces bittersweet
or semisweet chocolate,
chopped

1 cup (2 sticks) unsalted
butter, plus more for
greasing the cake pan

1 tablespoon pure vanilla
extract

11 large eggs, separated

¾ cup granulated sugar

½ cup teff

¼ cup confectioners' sugar,
for dusting

Whipped cream, vanilla ice
cream, or Yogurt Cream
(page 72), for serving
(optional)

Fresh raspberries, for
serving (optional)

I've said it before: teff isn't an easy grain to love. But being the stubborn, grain-obsessed person that I am, I was determined not to give up until I knew I'd left no grain unturned, teff among them. Enter the bright and beautiful mind of Emily, who worked with me on these recipes. At the end of our cooking days, Emily or I would make two *micheladas* (beer on ice with lime juice, in a salt-rimmed glass), sit outside on my tiny back patio, and talk grains. It was during one of these lime-soaked brainstorming sessions that Emily got the bright idea of using teff in the same way that polenta is used, to make a cake. That's what this is. There's no flour: just chocolate and teff (and of course butter and sugar—it is *cake*, after all).

The tiny grains of teff give a delightful little crunch to the cake, like poppy seeds in poppy seed cake. It's really chocolaty, but not too sweet, so, if you're that kind of person, you could totally justify eating this for breakfast. Whole-grain goodness aside, this is my new favorite chocolate cake, period.

You will need a 10-inch springform pan to make this. *Serves 8 to 10*

Adjust the oven racks so one is in the middle position and preheat the oven to 300°F. Grease the bottom and sides of a 10-inch springform pan with butter.

Put the chocolate and butter in a stainless-steel bowl and set the bowl over a pot of gently simmering water over medium heat to create a double boiler. (Make sure the water does not touch the bottom of the bowl; if it does, pour some out.) Heat the chocolate and butter together until they are melted and smooth, stirring occasionally to combine the two, and scraping down the sides of the bowl with a rubber spatula as they melt.

Remove the bowl from the heat, stir in the vanilla, and set aside to cool slightly.

In the bowl of a stand mixer fitted with the whisk attachment, beat the egg whites on medium speed until they're foamy. With the mixer running, rain in ½ cup of the granulated sugar and beat until the whites are shiny and hold stiff peaks. Gently, using a rubber spatula, transfer the beaten whites to a bowl. In the same mixer bowl (no need to clean it), beat the egg yolks until they begin to turn a pale yellow. Rain in the remaining ¼ cup granulated sugar and beat until the eggs are fluffy and the sugar has dissolved. Turn

recipe continues

Over-mixing will deflate the egg whites and result in a heavier cake

off the mixer. Add the chocolate-butter mixture to the egg yolks and gently fold them in with a rubber spatula. Carefully fold about one-quarter of the egg whites into the chocolate mixture, then transfer the chocolate–egg white mixture to the bowl with the remaining egg whites, mixing only as much as needed to combine. (The reason for the back-and-forth transferring here is that there likely won't be room in the bowl with the egg whites, initially.)

Pour the batter into the buttered pan and bake for 1 hour to 1 hour and 10 minutes, until a toothpick inserted into the center of the cake comes out clean; crumbs may stick to the toothpick, but it will not look like wet batter. (If you bake the cake until the toothpick comes out completely clean, the cake will be too dry.) Remove the cake from the oven and put it on a wire rack, or just set it away from the hot stove, to cool.

Unlatch and remove the sides of the springform pan. Leaving the cake on the bottom of the pan, lift onto a cake platter. Pour the confectioners' sugar into a fine-mesh strainer and gently dust the cake with the sugar. Slice and serve the cake on its own, or serve with the cream of your choice and fresh berries.

QUINOA INDIAN PUDDING

Unsalted butter, for
buttering the cups or
baking dishes

¼ cup white quinoa, rinsed

2 cups whole milk

¼ cup polenta (medium-
ground cornmeal)

¼ teaspoon kosher salt

½ teaspoon ground
cinnamon

½ teaspoon freshly grated
nutmeg (optional; use it if
you have it)

¼ teaspoon ground allspice
(optional; use it if you
have it)

¼ teaspoon ground ginger
(optional; use it if you
have it)

2 large eggs

½ cup molasses

Boiling water for the
bain-marie

Vanilla ice cream, for
serving

*A bain-marie, or water bath,
provides an even, gentle cooking
environment, which is ideal for
delicate concoctions like custard
and pudding.*

I first had Indian pudding at the now closed landmark New England restaurant Locke-Ober in Boston. I had never heard of Indian pudding, but I love trying foods I've never eaten, so I ordered it. What came to the table was a big, steaming bowl of pumpkin-colored, grainy-textured mush with a scoop of vanilla ice cream melting at its core. It looked like nothing I'd ever seen, but somehow it still managed to look like comfort food. (This was the early nineties, when any food not stacked in a ring mold had the potential to be filed under "comfort.") I asked the waitress what was in the dessert. "Pumpkin?" I guessed.

"Just cornmeal and molasses," she said.

It was hard to believe, but in fact, Indian pudding is every bit as simple as that waitress promised. I make mine with a combination of cornmeal and quinoa and what we've come to know as pumpkin pie spices. It makes a great alternative to the usual suspects for Thanksgiving dessert.

You will need six heatproof cups or individual baking dishes to make these. *Serves 6*

Adjust the oven racks so one is in the middle position and preheat the oven to 275°F. Butter the insides of six heatproof cups or individual baking dishes.

In a large saucepan, combine the quinoa and ½ cup water. Bring the water to a boil over high heat. Reduce heat to low, cover, and simmer the quinoa for 12 to 15 minutes, until all the water has been absorbed. Add the milk, increase the heat to medium-high, and heat until the milk starts to bubble around the edges of the pan.

Combine the polenta, salt, and spices in a medium bowl. Gradually add the polenta-spice mixture to the quinoa, stirring while you add it, and cook, stirring often to prevent the pudding from burning on the bottom of the pot, until it has thickened enough so that it coats the back of a wooden spoon or rubber spatula, about 15 minutes. Turn off the heat.

Beat the eggs in a small bowl. Gradually add ¼ cup of the pudding mixture to the bowl with the eggs, stirring continuously with a whisk to temper the eggs. Continue adding the pudding mixture gradually, stirring continuously, until you have added about half of it. Pour the egg-pudding mixture back into the saucepan with the remaining pudding and stir to combine. Stir in the molasses.

Pour the pudding into the buttered cups and place them in a baking dish. Fill the baking dish with boiling water to create a bain-marie. Put the baking dish in the oven and bake for 2 hours, or until the pudding pulls away from the sides of the cups and a skewer inserted into the center of the pudding comes out clean. Remove the baking dish from the oven and remove the puddings from the water bath. Let the pudding set for about 10 minutes before serving, but don't wait much longer, as it's essential that the pudding be warm to melt the scoop of ice cream that you are going to put on top.

DECONSTRUCTED ITALIAN EASTER PIE
with Wheat Berries and Honey

FOR THE CREAM

1 cup heavy cream

1 (10- to 12-ounce) package goat cheese, at room temperature

2 tablespoons sugar

1 orange

FOR THE TOPPING

1 cup honey

1 cup cooked wheat berries (see page 45; cooked to very tender, about 10 minutes longer than usual)

1 cup pistachios (or hazelnuts, or walnuts), toasted (see page 69)

G-Free Alternative: To make this gluten-free, substitute wild rice for the wheat berries.

Italian Easter Pie is essentially ricotta cheesecake with wheat berries mixed into the cheese. I've read about it for years but have never seen this pie in person, so I decided to make it myself. Seemed easy enough for a veteran pie baker like myself. Except that when they're baked wheat berries (and other chewy berries) become hard, like fish tank stones. No matter how long I soaked the grains or how much I overcooked them, what I ended up with each time was Italian pebble pie. Not one to make life more difficult than it needs to be (not when it comes to preparing dessert anyway), I decided to leave the wheat berries *outside* the pie, and then I turned my back on the pie structure altogether and just whipped the goat cheese into a fluffy, luscious cloud. Think of it as Italian Easter Pie, deconstructed. Or just think of it as simple, sweet, and delicious. *Serves 4-6*

To prepare the goat cheese "cream," beat the cream in a standing mixer fitted with the whisk attachment on medium speed until it begins to thicken and expand in volume, 4 to 5 minutes. Add the goat cheese and sugar and beat at medium speed until they are combined and no lumps of goat cheese remain, about 2 minutes. Using a Microplane, grate only the very outer layer of the orange zest into the bowl and gently fold it into the goat cheese cream. Cover and refrigerate until you are ready to serve the cream or for up to several days.

To prepare the topping, peel the orange and break it into segments; remove and discard the seeds and as much of the pith (the white stuff on the outside) as possible. Combine the honey with 1 cup water in a small saucepan and heat over medium just to melt the honey, about 5 minutes. Turn off the heat and stir in the orange segments, wheat berries, and nuts. Cool to room temperature.

To serve, spoon the whipped goat cheese into four or more bowls and spoon the wheat berry topping over it.

WHOLE-GRAIN WHITE CHOCOLATE COMPOST

2 cups flake cereal (cornflakes are the crunchiest, but bran and other flakes have an earthy appeal)

1 cup high-fiber bran cereal (such as All-Bran; or any cereal, the crunchier, the better)

1 cup salted pretzels or sesame sticks

½ cup buckwheat

¼ cup hulled roasted salted sunflower seeds

½ cup roasted salted pepitas (pumpkin seeds)

¼ cup dried currants (or finely chopped raisins or dried apricots)

1 tablespoon flaxseeds, poppy seeds, or hemp seeds (or a mix)

10 ounces white chocolate

Maldon, fleur de sel, or another flaky sea salt (optional)

This is my whole-grain, semi-healthy interpretation of white chocolate "trash." I came to the world of trash in a backward way: first, I made a crunchy whole-grain dessert snack consisting of whole-grain cereals, whole grains, nuts, and seeds bound with white chocolate. After I did, Emily said, "It's like trash!" In case you, too, are new to trash, it's an American confection in which a bunch of sweet and salty snack foods (pretzels, Oreos, M&M's—basically anything crunchy) are bound by melted white chocolate. Since my trash is on the earthier side, I call it "compost."

White chocolate gets a bad rap. People say it's "not really chocolate," but that isn't true. (What does it even mean?) White chocolate is made with as much as 45% cocoa butter, which is the fat extracted from cocoa beans. The rest is sugar and milk solids. What it doesn't have that brown chocolate *does* is cocoa solids, which is what makes chocolate brown. Look for quality brands of white chocolate, such as Valrhona, Callebaut, El Rey, or Guittard. *Serves 8 or more*

Line a large baking sheet with parchment paper or a Silpat baking mat.

Combine everything but the white chocolate and salt in a big bowl.

Put the white chocolate in a stainless-steel bowl and set the bowl over a pot of gently simmering water over medium heat to create a double boiler. (Make sure the water does not touch the bottom of the bowl; if it does, pour some out.) Melt the white chocolate, stirring and scraping down the sides of the bowl with a rubber spatula so the white chocolate doesn't scorch, which it does easily.

Scrape the melted white chocolate into the bowl with the cereals and seeds.

Use a rubber spatula or your hands to fold everything together so the white chocolate coats all the other ingredients.

Dump the compost onto the prepared baking sheet and use your fingers to spread it out into a thin, lacy layer. Sprinkle a couple big pinches of sea salt on top and put the baking sheet in the refrigerator until the white chocolate hardens, at least 30 minutes.

To serve, break the compost into manageable shards and stack them on a plate.

GOAT'S MILK RICE PUDDING
with Cinnamon and Raisins

1 cup long-grain brown
rice, rinsed

1 cinnamon stick (optional)

¼ teaspoon kosher salt

4 cups goat's milk (or
cow's milk)

1 vanilla bean pod
(optional)

1 teaspoon pure vanilla
extract (2 teaspoons if you
aren't using a vanilla bean)

½ cup raw or granulated
sugar

¼ cup to ½ cup black
raisins

Ground cinnamon, for
sprinkling

I'm a pretty adventurous eater, but I was still squeamish about the idea of goat's milk until I made the connection that *cajeta*—Mexico's version of *dulce de leche*—is made with goat's milk. Goat's milk has less lactose than cow's milk, which makes it easier to digest, so even though I am lactose challenged, I can handle this milky dessert *no problema*. If, despite my best efforts, I have not sold you on goat's milk, make this with cow's milk. I got the idea to pour the pudding out onto a platter to cool and serve from a recipe of the venerable Spanish cook José Andrés. The first time I made it that way, I felt like an old Spanish *abuela*, which indeed I have somewhere deep in my ancestral past.

There's a fine line between dessert and breakfast that, for me, is defined by quantity of sugar. To make this for breakfast, use half as much sugar. *Serves 4 to 6*

Combine 2 cups water, the rice, cinnamon stick (if you're using it), and salt in a large saucepan. Bring the water to a boil over high heat. Reduce the heat to maintain a simmer and cook the rice for 10 minutes. Add the milk. If you are using a vanilla bean, split it in half with a sharp knife and scrape the tiny seeds out with the dull edge of the knife. Add the seeds and the pod to the pot. Increase the heat to medium-high and heat until the milk begins to bubble around the edges. Reduce the heat to maintain a simmer and cook, stirring often so the milk doesn't burn on the bottom of the pot and a skin doesn't form on the top, until the rice is tender and the pudding is thick, about 40 minutes. Stir in the vanilla extract and raisins and cook the pudding for 5 minutes more to soften the raisins. If the pudding is thick but the rice needs more cooking time, add water and keep cooking.

Pour the rice pudding out onto a platter to cool. Sprinkle with cinnamon and serve family-style, with bowls and spoons.

DARK CHOCOLATE FARRO GOOP
with Toasted Walnuts and Steamed Cream

4 ounces dark chocolate, chopped

2 cups heavy cream

2 tablespoons brewed coffee (hot or cold)

¼ teaspoon kosher salt

1 cup cooked farro

1 heaping cup walnut halves, toasted (see page 69)

G-Free Alternative: If you want gluten-free goop, make this with whole oat groats.

Once upon a time, at a Los Angeles restaurant now closed, there was a dessert called a Warm Brownie Sundae, which wasn't a brownie at all, but a small, messy mountain of hot, dark-chocolaty deliciousness surrounded by a moat of steamed cream. As great as the dark-chocolaty stuff was, what made it truly spectacular was that it was floating in this river of rich, warm cream. Over the years, I've used that presentation to serve many desserts, that might otherwise have been assigned to a scoop of vanilla ice cream. This dessert is my whole-grain version of that; it's a sort of deconstructed brownie using whole farro bound by chocolate. Warning: small portion advisory alert in effect. *Serves 6*

Put the chocolate and ½ cup of the cream in a stainless-steel bowl and set the bowl over a pot of gently simmering water over medium heat to create a double boiler. (Make sure the water does not touch the bottom of the bowl; if it does, pour some out.) Melt the chocolate with the cream. Turn off the heat and stir in the coffee and salt. Add the farro and break half of the walnuts so they fall in big pieces into the bowl; stir to combine.

Steam or warm the remaining 1½ cups cream (see sidebar).

Scoop the chocolaty farro into four (or more) deep bowls. Pour the steamed cream around the edges of the bowls and sprinkle with the remaining walnuts.

"STEAMING" MILK OR CREAM

I am not a gadget person, nor do I indulge in cappuccinos (outside of Italy), so it's no wonder that I do not own a milk steamer. The problem is, I *do* love steamed milk and steamed cream, so I learned a way to achieve the same effect, without having one more kitchen tool to find a place for. Here's how:

If you want your milk or cream warm, which you probably do, warm it. (I think a stove is a great invention for this job, but I know some people prefer to use a microwave.) Pour your warm or cold milk or cream into a heatproof jar or a shaker. (Whatever vessel you choose, it must be wide enough to plunge a wire whisk into.) Plunge a wire whisk into the vessel of milk or cream and grasp the whisk handle between the palms of both hands; it will look like you clapped your hands and a whisk handle got stuck between them. Slide your hands back and forth in opposite directions so the whisk spins. Keep doing this, and within minutes you will have "steamed" milk or cream.

TEMPERING EGGS

Tempering eggs is the process by which you very gradually and gently raise the temperature of eggs to meet the temperature of the hot liquid to which they are being married. Otherwise, the heat from the liquid will cook the eggs and you'll end up with little bits of scrambled eggs in your mix.

TOASTED MILLET FROZEN CUSTARD
with Pan-Seared Fruit

½ cup plus 2 tablespoons millet

2 cups milk

2 cups heavy whipping cream

¾ cup sugar

¼ teaspoon kosher salt

4 large egg yolks, lightly beaten

Pan-Seared Fruit (recipe follows)

Not just birdseed anymore: Tiny, toasted millet grains give the perfect crunch to this rich, eggy, custard-based ice cream. Custard refers to milk and cream cooked with egg until it's thick and (yes) custardy. Ice cream that is made from egg yolks, which is the traditional French way of making ice cream (and which includes the majority of premium ice cream sold in the U.S.), is frozen custard. This is that, and I serve it with pan-seared seasonal fruit, but obviously you should eat it however you like to eat ice cream. Homemade ice cream doesn't contain stabilizers or have as much air in it as commercial ice cream, so completely frozen, it's hard as a rock. The best way to enjoy it is fresh from the ice cream maker, when it's still soft, or after it's been in the freezer long enough to set up slightly. *Serves 4 to 6*

Toast the millet in a skillet over medium heat, shaking the pan continuously so the grains don't burn, for 2 to 3 minutes, until the grains are barely golden. Set aside to cool to room temperature.

Combine the milk, cream, sugar, and salt in a medium saucepan and heat over medium-high heat, stirring often, until the liquid begins to bubble around the edges. Turn off the heat and gradually add a ladleful of the hot cream mixture to the bowl with the eggs to temper them, whisking continuously. Continue adding the cream mixture gradually, stirring with a whisk continuously, until you have added about half of it. Pour the egg mixture back into the saucepan with the cream and cook over medium-low heat, stirring continuously with a wooden spoon or rubber spatula, until the custard is thick enough to coat the back of the spoon or spatula. Turn off the heat and stir in ½ cup of the millet. Cover the custard with plastic wrap, gently pressing the plastic against the surface of the custard to prevent a skin from forming, and set aside to cool to room temperature. Refrigerate the ice cream base overnight or for at least 2 hours.

Spin the chilled custard in an ice cream maker according to the manufacturer's instructions. Serve the ice cream straight from the ice cream maker, or transfer it to a container, freeze, and serve before it becomes rock hard.

Serve the ice cream with the fruit on top and sprinkle with the remaining millet.

recipe continues

Pan-Seared Fruit

Searing fruit brings out its natural sweetness, turning even fairly ordinary fruit into a delicious dessert in minutes. Use this recipe to cook any fruit that is in season. I'm sure I do not have to tell you, on the last page of this book, that in-season fruit, purchased from a farmers' market, is going to be infinitely sweeter and more flavorful than out-of-season, industrially-raised fruit picked unripe and shipped in from faraway lands, and sold at your average grocery store.

Enjoy. *Serves 4*

¼ cup (½ stick) unsalted butter

2 tablespoons raw or granulated sugar (optional)

2 ripe peaches, nectarines, or apricots (halved lengthwise and pitted); or 6 figs (halved lengthwise); or 2 pears (quartered and cored); or 2 bananas or 1 pineapple, peeled and sliced ¾-inch thick

Melt the butter in a medium skillet over medium heat and cook until it just begins to foam, but do not let it brown. Sprinkle the sugar over the surface of the pan, if you are using it. Lay the fruit cut-side down in the pan and cook until the side touching the pan is caramelized, about 3 minutes. Turn and cook the other side until caramelized.

Spoon the brown butter remaining in the pan over the fruit and serve with ice cream, yogurt, or porridge.

ACKNOWLEDGMENTS

Thank you…

To Janis Donnaud, the most demanding, supportive, honest, and hardest working agent I could ask for. I'm so glad she's on my side.

To Nancy Silverton, a great (and I do mean *great*) teacher and friend who I have had the privilege of learning from and cooking with for almost 15 years. Nancy called me almost daily as I was writing this book to share grain bowl inspiration she'd seen in other restaurants, magazines, or that just came out of the wellspring that is her imagination. And this from someone who doesn't even *eat* grains.

To Beatriz da Costa for the stunning photos. Beatriz is a true artist, and it was a real pleasure to see her process—and her photos.

To Susan Spungen, brilliant genius and my friend of over two decades, who does some kind of magic to make food look delicious, effortless, and, best yet, *un-styled* on the page. Susan's work defined food styling for this generation and the fact that she agreed to style my book was a great honor and gift.

To Susan and Bea's crew, including Laura Kinsey and Pia Moore, who, for two straight weeks, worked above and beyond in their pursuit of beauty and perfection.

To prop-master Helen Crowther, who was very generous and big hearted with her stunning props.

To the team at Grand Central Life & Style, most especially Brittany McInerney for her tireless efforts at the endless onion of editing, and Karen Murgolo for believing in my book to begin with.

To Amy Sly for taking direction from all angles and turning it into a gorgeous and lively book.

To my sister Christy for her occasional trips to the grocery store, for letting me raid her fridge even when she didn't know I was doing it, and for eating so many grains even when she may not have wanted to.

To the entire Chino clan for their continuous support and inspiring vegetables.

To Adriene Hughes, for the pretty author photo and for the photography lessons she gave Emily and me as we were working on the book.

And most of all, thanks to Emily Corliss, who worked with such focus, attention to detail, and dedication in helping me to make every recipe in these pages as delicious and home-cook friendly as they could be. Emily has such a smart sensibility when it comes to food; she never suggests anything I would find silly or unnecessary or just plain weird. Instead, it was all fun, with regular flashes of total brilliance (see Lamb Meatballs). She worked on this book as if it were her own, which is the dream, isn't it?

INDEX

acorn squash
  in Brazilian Bowl with Quick-Cooked
    Collards and Aji, 208
  in Farmers' Market Bowl with Yogurt
    Green Goddess and Salty Pepitas, 123
Aji, 208
  Brazilian Bowl with Quick-Cooked
    Collards and, 206
almonds
  toasting, 69
  Chinese Chicken Salad with Toasted
    Almonds and Crispy Rice, 109
  Homemade Nut Milk, 65
  in Slow-Cooked Brown Rice and
    Quinoa Porridge, 68
  in Winter Wild Rice Salad with Dates
    and Parmesan, 106
amaranth
  about, 34
  Four Grain "Nutella" Porridge with
    Toasted Hazelnuts and Jam, 64
Antipasto Rice Salad with Tuna and Egg,
  Italian, 95
apples
  Sourmash Apple Crisp with Whole-
    Grain Crisp Topping, 217
  Spiced Apple Breakfast Farro with Yogurt
    Cream, 72
  Sticky Rice and Apple Slaw, 163
Asian Bowl, Build Your Own, 136
Asian Breakfast Porridge with Turkey
  Meatballs, 76
asparagus
  in Chino Ranch Vegetable Bowl with
    Kale Pistachio Pesto and Bagna
    Cauda, 154
  in Sambal Tofu Quinoa Bowl with
    Sesame Spring Veggies, 119
avocados
  about, 86
  Broccolini and Sprout Salad with Poppy
    Seed Dressing and Avocado, 111
  in Japanese Breakfast with Spinach,
    Salmon, and Sweet Miso Dressing, 61
  Mole Teff and Chicken with Avocado
    and Crema, 174
  in Quinoa Huevos Rancheros Bowl, 83
  Salmon Poke Bowl with Brown Rice
    and Edamame, 130
  Spicy Tuna Tartare with Brown Sushi
    Rice and Avocado, 126

  in Sunday Night Detox Bowl with
    Roasted Broccoli and Ponzu, 186

Baba-G, 171
  Pomegranate Tabbouleh with Crunchy
    Falafel, Tahini Sauce, and, 167
bacon
  in Pastrami and Rye Berry Hash with
    Mustard Greens and Pickled Mustard
    Seeds, 73
  in Quick and Easy Breakfast Fried
    Quinoa, 53
  Sorghum Risotto Primavera with Bacon
    and Burrata, 205
Bagna Cauda, 156
  Chino Ranch Vegetable Bowl with Kale
    Pistachio Pesto and Bagna Cauda, 154
Baja BBQ Shrimp Bowl with Corn Rice,
  199
baking sheets, 26
Balsamic Vinaigrette, 96
Bananas and Poppy Seeds, Coconut Millet
  Porridge with, 80
barley
  about, 34–35
  in Broccolini and Sprout Salad with
    Poppy Seed Dressing and Avocado, 111
beef
  about, 22
  Five-Spice Riblets with Sticky Rice and
    Apple Slaw, 160
  Korean Short Ribs with Kimchi Rice,
    196
  in Ultimate Burrito Bowl, 192
Beet, Red, and Quinoa Salad with
  Hazelnuts and Goat Cheese, 96
Berry Crisp with Whole-Grain Crisp
  Topping, Mixed, 215
Black Beans, 84
  in Baja BBQ Shrimp Bowl with Corn
    Rice, 199
  in Brazilian Bowl with Quick-Cooked
    Collards and Ají, 206
  in Quinoa Huevos Rancheros Bowl, 83
  in Ultimate Burrito Bowl, 192
black rice
  about, 35
  Burnt Vegetable Bowl with Black Rice
    and Lentils and Tahini Sauce, 147
  Coconut Black and Wild Rice Pudding
    with Mangoes and Macadamia

  Nuts, 212
  in Sambal Tofu Quinoa Bowl with
    Sesame Spring Veggies, 119
blenders, 26
bocconcini, in Umbrian Farro and Bean
  Salad with Celery Leaf Pesto, and
  Mozzarella, 103
Boiled Eggs, 59–60
  Italian Antipasto Rice Salad with Tuna
    and Egg, 95
  in Japanese Breakfast with Spinach,
    Salmon, and Sweet Miso Dressing, 61
Bone Marrow and Parsley Salad, Graveyard
  Rice with, 151
bowls, stocking, 27
bran cereal, in Whole-Grain White
  Chocolate Compost, 225
Brazilian Bowl with Quick-Cooked
  Collards and Aji, 206
Brazilian Rice, 207
breakfast bowls, index listing, 49
Broccoli and Ponzu, Sunday Night Detox
  Bowl with Roasted, 186
Broccolini
  Broccolini and Sprout Salad with Poppy
    Seed Dressing and Avocado, 111
  in Burnt Vegetable Bowl with Black Rice
    and Lentils and Tahini Sauce, 147
Broccolini and Sprout Salad with Poppy
  Seed Dressing and Avocado, 111
brown rice
  about long-grain, 35–36
  about short-grain, 36
  Asian Breakfast Porridge with Turkey
    Meatballs, 76
  Butternut Squash Risotto with Slow-
    Cooked Kale, 149
  Chile En Nogada Bowl with Turkey
    Picadillo and Walnut Crema, 178
  Chinese Chicken Salad with Toasted
    Almonds and Crispy Rice, 109
  Coconut Curry Rice Bowl with Green
    Vegetables and Sweet Potatoes, 164
  Ginger Scallion Rice, 135
  Goat's Milk Rice Pudding with
    Cinnamon Raisins, 227
  Graveyard Rice with Bone Marrow and
    Parsley Salad, 151
  Italian Antipasto Rice Salad with Tuna
    and Egg, 95

Japanese Breakfast with Spinach, Salmon, and Sweet Miso Dressing, 61
Kimchi Rice, 198
Mexican Restaurant Rice, 195
Rice Bowl with Poached Egg, Slow-Roasted Tomatoes, and Avocado, 55
Slow-Cooked Brown Rice and Quinoa Porridge, 68
Sorghum Risotto Primavera with Bacon and Burrata, 205
Spicy Tuna Tartare with Brown Sushi Rice and Avocado, 126
Sticky Rice and Apple Slaw, 163
Sunday Night Detox Bowl with Roasted Broccoli and Ponzu, 186
Vietnamese Bowl with Sweet and Tangy Vinaigrette, 120
Brown Sushi Rice, 126
Spicy Tuna Tartare with Avocado and, 126
Brussels sprouts
in Coconut Curry Rice Bowl with Green Vegetables and Sweet Potatoes, 164
in Farmers' Market Bowl with Yogurt Green Goddess and Salty Pepitas, 123
Shaved Brussels Sprouts with Spelt, Walnuts, and Pecorino, 98
buckwheat
about, 37
Rosemary Buckwheat Crunch with Fresh Ricotta, 70
in Whole-Grain Crisp Topping, 216
in Whole-Grain White Chocolate Compost, 225
Build Your Own
about, 16
Asian Bowl, 136
Farmers' Market-Inspired Bowl, 153
Mexican Bowl, 191
Middle Eastern Bowl, 172
bulgur wheat
about, 37
in Pomegranate Tabbouleh, 168
Burnt Vegetable Bowl with Black Rice and Lentils and Tahini Sauce, 147
Burrata, Sorghum Risotto Primavera with Bacon and, 205
Burrito Bowl, Ultimate, 192
Butternut Squash Risotto with Slow-Cooked Kale, 149

cabbage
in Baja BBQ Shrimp Bowl with Corn Rice, 199
in Chinese Chicken Salad with Toasted Almonds and Crispy Rice, 109

in Kimchi Rice, 198
in Sambal Tofu Quinoa Bowl with Sesame Spring Veggies, 119
in Sesame Duck and Wild Rice Salad, 100
in Sticky Rice and Apple Slaw, 163
in Vietnamese Bowl with Sweet and Tangy Vinaigrette, 120
Caesar Bowl with Quinoa and Kale, Warm Chicken, 131
Caesar Dressing, 132
Cake, Flourless Chocolate Teff, 218
carrots
in Farmers' Market Bowl with Yogurt Green Goddess and Salty Pepitas, 123
in Moroccan Millet with Braised Root Vegetables and Harissa, 157
Pickled Vegetables, 135
Rainbow Carrot Salad with Millet, Feta, and Lemon Yogurt Dressing, 93
cashews. See also Chipotle Cashew Crema
Homemade Nut Milk, 65
Cauliflower and Chickpea Curry with Savory Yogurt and Millet, Indian, 202
Celery Leaf Pesto, 104
Umbrian Farro and Bean Salad with Celery Leaf Pesto, and Mozzarella, 103
chicken
about, 23
Chicken Satay Bowl with Coconut Rice, 138
Chinese Chicken Salad with Toasted Almonds and Crispy Rice, 109
Mole Teff and Chicken with Avocado and Crema, 174
in Ultimate Burrito Bowl, 192
in Vietnamese Bowl with Sweet and Tangy Vinaigrette, 120
Warm Chicken Caesar Bowl with Quinoa and Kale, 131
Chicken or Tofu Satay Bowl with Coconut Rice, 138
Chicken Stock, 78
chickpeas
in Hummus, 185
Indian Cauliflower and Chickpea Curry with Savory Yogurt and Millet, 202
in Italian-Style Beans, 104
in Moroccan Millet with Braised Root Vegetables and Harissa, 157
in Pomegranate Tabbouleh with Crunchy Falafel, Baba-G, and Tahini Sauce, 167
Chile En Nogada Bowl with Turkey Picadillo and Walnut Crema, 178
Chinese Chicken Salad with Toasted Almonds and Crispy Rice, 109

Chino Ranch Vegetable Bowl with Kale Pistachio Pesto and Bagna Cauda, 154
Chipotle Cashew Crema, 193
Ultimate Burrito Bowl with, 192
chocolate
Dark Chocolate Farro Goop with Toasted Walnuts and Steamed Cream, 228
Flourless Chocolate Teff Cake, 218
Four Grain "Nutella" Porridge with Toasted Hazelnuts and Jam, 64
Whole-Grain White Chocolate Compost, 225
coconut
Coconut Black and Wild Rice Pudding with Mangoes and Macadamia Nuts, 212
Coconut Curry Rice Bowl with Green Vegetables and Sweet Potatoes, 164
Coconut Millet Porridge with Bananas and Poppy Seeds, 80
Sweet and Salty Granola with Toasted Coconut and Pecans, 75
Coconut Black and Wild Rice Pudding with Mangoes and Macadamia Nuts, 212
Coconut Millet Porridge with Bananas and Poppy Seeds, 80
Coconut Rice, 140
Chicken or Tofu Satay Bowl with, 138
collard greens
Brazilian Bowl with Quick-Cooked Collards and Ají, 206
in Quick and Easy Breakfast Fried Quinoa, 53
Corn Farrotto with Brown Butter and Sweet Burst Tomatoes, Summer, 144
cornflakes
in Sweet and Salty Granola with Toasted Coconut and Pecans, 75
in Whole-Grain White Chocolate Compost, 225
Corn Rice, 200
Baja BBQ Shrimp Bowl with, 199
crisps
Mixed Berry Crisp with Whole-Grain Crisp Topping, 215
Sourmash Apple Crisp with Whole-Grain Crisp Topping, 217
Crispy Fried Eggs, 58
in Pastrami and Rye Berry Hash with Mustard Greens and Pickled Mustard Seeds, 73
cucumbers
in Chicken or Tofu Satay Bowl with Coconut Rice, 138

in Pomegranate Tabbouleh, 168
in Sorghum Greek Salad, 105

Dark Chocolate Farro Goop with Toasted
Walnuts and Steamed Cream, 228
Dates, Winter Wild Rice Salad with
Parmesan and, 106
Deconstructed Italian Easter Pie with
Wheat Berries and Honey, 224
dessert bowls, index listing, 211
Duck and Wild Rice Salad, Sesame, 100
Dutch ovens, 27

Edamame, Salmon Poke with Brown Rice,
130
eggplants, in Baba-G, 171
eggs
about, 23
tempering tip, 229
Boiled. See Boiled Eggs
Crispy Fried. See Crispy Fried Eggs
in Farmers' Market Bowl with Yogurt
Green Goddess and Salty Pepitas, 123
Italian Antipasto Rice Salad with Tuna
and Egg, 95
Poached. See Poached Eggs
in Quick and Easy Breakfast Fried
Quinoa, 53
in Quinoa Huevos Rancheros Bowl, 83
in Spiced Apple Breakfast Farro with
Yogurt Cream, 72
entertaining with grain bowls, 17
equipment, 25–31

Falafel, Baba-G, and Tahini Sauce,
Pomegranate Tabbouleh with Crunchy,
167
Farmers' Market Bowl with Yogurt Green
Goddess and Salty Pepitas, 123
Farmers' Market-Inspired Bowl, Build Your
Own, 153
farro
about, 37–38
in Chino Ranch Vegetable Bowl with
Kale Pistachio Pesto and Bagna Cauda,
154
Dark Chocolate Farro Goop with
Toasted Walnuts and Steamed Cream,
228
Spiced Apple Breakfast Farro with Yogurt
Cream, 72
Summer Corn Farrotto with Brown
Butter and Sweet Burst Tomatoes, 144
Umbrian Farro and Bean Salad with
Celery Leaf Pesto, and Mozzarella, 103
fennel
in Quinoa and Poached Salmon Salad

with Confetti Vegetables, 90
in Winter Wild Rice Salad with Dates
and Parmesan, 106
feta
about, 55
Rainbow Carrot Salad with Millet, Feta,
and Lemon Yogurt Dressing, 93
Rice Bowl with Poached Egg, Slow-
Roasted Tomatoes, and Feta, 55
in Sorghum Greek Salad, 105
Five-Spice Riblets with Sticky Rice and
Apple Slaw, 160
Flourless Chocolate Teff Cake, 218
food processors, mini, 26
Four Grain "Nutella" Porridge with
Toasted Hazelnuts and Jam, 64
freekeh
about, 38–39
in Pomegranate Tabbouleh, 168
Fried Eggs. See Crispy Fried Eggs
fruit. See also specific fruits
about, 19–20
Toasted Millet Frozen Custard with Pan-
Seared Fruit, 230

Ginger Scallion Rice, 135
Glazed Pork Belly with Pickled
Vegetables and, 133
in Sunday Night Detox Bowl with
Roasted Broccoli and Ponzu, 186
Ginger Vinaigrette, 110
Glazed Pork Belly with Ginger Scallion
Rice and Pickled Vegetables, 133
gloves, food-handling, 27
goat cheese
in Deconstructed Italian Easter Pie with
Wheat Berries and Honey, 224
Red Beet and Quinoa Salad with
Hazelnuts and Goat Cheese, 96
Goat's Milk Rice Pudding with Cinnamon
Raisins, 227
Grandmother Birdie's Oatmeal Cocktail
with Raisins and Salty Sunflower Seeds,
50
Granola, Sweet and Salty, with Toasted
Coconut and Pecans, 75
grass-fed beef. See beef
Graveyard Rice with Bone Marrow and
Parsley Salad, 151
Greek Salad, Sorghum, 105
green beans
in Burnt Vegetable Bowl with Black Rice
and Lentils and Tahini Sauce, 147
in Chino Ranch Vegetable Bowl with
Kale Pistachio Pesto and Bagna Cauda,
154

Green Goddess Dressing. See Yogurt
Green Goddess
greens. See collard greens; kale; Mustard
Greens
griddles, cast-iron, 26
grill pans, 26

Halloumi, Spiced Rice and Lentils with
Seared, 141
hazelnuts
toasting, 69
Four Grain "Nutella" Porridge with
Toasted Hazelnuts and Jam, 64
Red Beet and Quinoa Salad with
Hazelnuts and Goat Cheese, 96
Huevos Rancheros Bowl, Quinoa, 83
Hummus, 185
Mezze Bowl with Pomegranate-Glazed
Lamb Meatballs, Tzatziki, and, 183

Indian Cauliflower and Chickpea Curry
with Savory Yogurt and Millet, 202
Indian Pudding, Quinoa, 222
Italian Antipasto Rice Salad with Tuna and
Egg, 95
Italian Easter Pie with Wheat Berries and
Honey, Deconstructed, 224
Italian-Style Beans, 104
Umbrian Farro and Bean Salad with
Celery Leaf Pesto, and Mozzarella, 103

Japanese Breakfast with Spinach, Salmon,
and Sweet Miso
Dressing, 61

kale
Butternut Squash Risotto with Slow-
Cooked Kale, 149
Chino Ranch Vegetable Bowl with Kale
Pistachio Pesto and Bagna Cauda, 154
in Coconut Curry Rice Bowl with
Green Vegetables and Sweet Potatoes,
164
in Spiced Rice and Lentils with Seared
Halloumi, 141
Warm Chicken Caesar Bowl with
Quinoa and Kale, 131
Kale Pistachio Pesto, 156
Chino Ranch Vegetable Bowl with, 154
kaniwa, about, 39
Khorasan wheat
about, 39–40
in Farmers' Market Bowl with Yogurt
Green Goddess and Salty Pepitas, 123
Kimchi Rice, 198
Korean Short Ribs with, 196
kitchen equipment, 25–31

kitchen staples, 19–23
knives, 30
Korean Short Ribs with Kimchi Rice, 196

lamb
about, 21–22
Mezze Bowl with Pomegranate-Glazed Lamb Meatballs, Hummus, and Tzatziki, 183
Lemon Vinaigrette, 90
Lemon Yogurt Dressing, 94
Rainbow Carrot Salad with Millet, Feta, and, 93
lentils
Burnt Vegetable Bowl with Black Rice and Lentils and Tahini Sauce, 147
Spiced Rice and Lentils, 143

Macadamia Nuts, Coconut Black and Wild Rice Pudding with Mangoes and, 212
main bowls, index listing, 116–17
mandolines, 25–26
Mangoes and Macadamia Nuts, Coconut Black and Wild Rice Pudding with, 212
meatballs
Asian Breakfast Porridge with Turkey Meatballs, 76
Mezze Bowl with Pomegranate-Glazed Lamb Meatballs, Hummus, and Tzatziki, 183
Mexican Bowl, Build Your Own, 191
Mexican elbows, 31
Mexican Restaurant Rice, 195
in Ultimate Burrito Bowl, 192
Mezze Bowl with Pomegranate-Glazed Lamb Meatballs, Hummus, and Tzatziki, 183
microplanes, 25
Middle Eastern Bowl, Build Your Own, 172
millet
about, 40
Coconut Millet Porridge with Bananas and Poppy Seeds, 80
in Four Grain "Nutella" Porridge with Toasted Hazelnuts and Jam, 64
Millet Polenta with Wild Mushrooms and Parmesan, 129
Moroccan Millet with Braised Root Vegetables and Harissa, 157
Rainbow Carrot Salad with Millet, Feta, and Lemon Yogurt Dressing, 93
Toasted Millet Frozen Custard with Pan-Seared Fruit, 230
Millet Polenta with Wild Mushrooms and Parmesan, 129

Mixed Berry Crisp with Whole-Grain Crisp Topping, 215
Mole Teff and Chicken with Avocado and Crema, 174
Moroccan Millet, 159
with Braised Root Vegetables and Harissa, 157
Mozzarella, Umbrian Farro and Bean Salad with Celery Leaf Pesto, and, 103
Mushrooms, Millet Polenta with Parmesan and Wild, 129
Mustard Greens and Pickled Mustard Seeds, Pastrami and Rye Berry Hash with, 73

"Nutella" Porridge with Toasted Hazelnuts and Jam, Four Grain, 64
Nut Milk, 65
Four Grain "Nutella" Porridge with Toasted Hazelnuts and Jam, 64
nuts. See also hazelnuts; pecans; walnuts
toasting, 69
in Slow-Cooked Brown Rice and Quinoa Porridge, 68

Oatmeal Cocktail with Raisins and Salty Sunflower Seeds, Grandmother Birdie's, 50
oats
about, 40, 42
Grandmother Birdie's Oatmeal Cocktail with Raisins and Salty Sunflower Seeds, 50
in Sweet and Salty Granola with Toasted Coconut and Pecans, 75
Orange Vinaigrette, 106

Pad Thai with Tofu and Shrimp, Red Rice, 182
pans, 26, 29
Pan-Seared Fruit, 233
Toasted Millet Frozen Custard with, 230
Parmesan cheese
Millet Polenta with Wild Mushrooms and Parmesan, 129
Winter Wild Rice Salad with Dates and Parmesan, 106
Parsley Salad, Graveyard Rice with Bone Marrow and, 151
parsnips
in Graveyard Rice with Bone Marrow and Parsley Salad, 151
in Moroccan Millet with Braised Root Vegetables and Harissa, 157
Pastrami and Rye Berry Hash with Mustard Greens and Pickled Mustard Seeds, 73

PB&J Porridge, 68
pecans
toasting, 69
Sweet and Salty Granola with Toasted Coconut and Pecans, 75
Pecorino, Shaved Brussels Sprouts with Spelt, Walnuts, and, 98
pepitas (pumpkin seeds)
toasting, 69
Farmers' Market Bowl with Yogurt Green Goddess and Salty Pepitas, 123
in Whole-Grain White Chocolate Compost, 225
pepperoncini, in Italian Antipasto Rice Salad with Tuna and Egg, 95
Pepperoncini Vinaigrette, 95
Pesto
Celery Leaf, 104
Kale Pistachio, 156
Pickled Mustard Seeds, 74
Pastrami and Rye Berry Hash with Mustard Greens and Pickled Mustard Seeds, 73
Pickled Vegetables, 135
Glazed Pork Belly with Ginger Scallion Rice and, 133
in Japanese Breakfast with Spinach, Salmon, and Sweet Miso Dressing, 61
pine nuts
toasting, 69
in Spiced Rice and Lentils with Seared Halloumi, 141
Poached Eggs, 59
in Asian Breakfast Porridge with Turkey Meatballs, 76
Rice Bowl with Poached Egg, Slow-Roasted Tomatoes, and Feta, 55
Poached Salmon, 63
in Japanese Breakfast with Spinach, Salmon, and Sweet Miso Dressing, 61
Quinoa and Poached Salmon Salad with Confetti Vegetables, 90
Poblano Rice, 180
in Chile En Nogada Bowl with Turkey Picadillo and Walnut Crema, 178
Poke, Salmon, with Edamame and Avocado, 130
polenta
Millet Polenta with Wild Mushrooms and Parmesan, 129
in Quinoa Indian Pudding, 222
pomegranates, seeding tips, 168
Pomegranate Tabbouleh, 168
with Crunchy Falafel, Baba-G, and Tahini Sauce, 167
Ponzu Sauce, 189

Sunday Night Detox Bowl with Roasted
     Broccoli and, 186
Poppy Seed Dressing, 112
     Broccolini and Sprout Salad with
          Avocado and, 111
**Poppy Seeds, Coconut Millet Porridge
     with Bananas and, 80**
pork
     about, 21
     Glazed Pork Belly with Ginger Scallion
          Rice and Pickled Vegetables, 133
pots, 26, 29
pudding
     Coconut Black and Wild Rice Pudding
          with Mangoes and Macadamia
          Nuts, 212
     Goat's Milk Rice Pudding with
          Cinnamon Raisins, 227
     Quinoa Indian Pudding, 222

**Quick and Easy Breakfast Fried Quinoa,
     53**
quinoa
     about, 42
     in Chile En Nogada Bowl with Turkey
          Picadillo and Walnut Crema, 178
     Corn Quinoa, 200
     in Four Grain "Nutella" Porridge with
          Toasted Hazelnuts and Jam, 64
     Quick and Easy Breakfast Fried Quinoa,
          53
     Quinoa and Poached Salmon Salad with
          Confetti Vegetables, 90
     Quinoa Huevos Rancheros Bowl, 83
     Quinoa Indian Pudding, 222
     Red Beet and Quinoa Salad with
          Hazelnuts and Goat Cheese, 96
     Sambal Tofu Quinoa Bowl with Sesame
          Spring Veggies, 119
     Slow-Cooked Brown Rice and Quinoa
          Porridge, 68
     in Vietnamese Bowl with Sweet and
          Tangy Vinaigrette, 120
     Warm Chicken Caesar Bowl with
          Quinoa and Kale, 131
**Quinoa and Poached Salmon Salad with
     Confetti Vegetables, 90**
Quinoa Huevos Rancheros Bowl, 83
Quinoa Indian Pudding, 222

radicchio
     in Farmers' Market Bowl with Yogurt
          Green Goddess and Salty Pepitas, 123
     in Italian Antipasto Rice Salad with Tuna
          and Egg, 95
     in Red Beet and Quinoa Salad with
          Hazelnuts and Goat Cheese, 96

radishes
     Pickled Vegetables, 135
     in Quinoa and Poached Salmon Salad
          with Confetti Vegetables, 90
     in Sorghum Greek Salad, 105
**Rainbow Carrot Salad with Millet, Feta,
     and Lemon Yogurt Dressing, 93**
raisins
     Goat's Milk Rice Pudding with
          Cinnamon Raisins, 227
     Grandmother Birdie's Oatmeal Cocktail
          with Raisins and Salty Sunflower
          Seeds, 50
     in Rainbow Carrot Salad with Millet,
          Feta, and Lemon Yogurt Dressing, 93
**Red Beet and Quinoa Salad with
     Hazelnuts and Goat Cheese, 96**
red rice
     about, 42–43
     Red Rice Pad Thai with Tofu and
          Shrimp, 182
**Red Rice Pad Thai with Tofu and Shrimp,
     182**
**Rice Bowl with Poached Egg, Slow-
     Roasted Tomatoes, and Feta, 55**
**Ricotta, Rosemary Buckwheat Crunch
     with Fresh, 70**
risotto
     Butternut Squash Risotto with Slow-
          Cooked Kale, 149
     Sorghum Risotto Primavera with Bacon
          and Burrata, 205
**Rosemary Buckwheat Crunch with Fresh
     Ricotta, 70**
rye
     about, 43
     Pastrami and Rye Berry Hash with
          Mustard Greens and Pickled Mustard
          Seeds, 73

salad bowls, index listing, 89
salad dressings and vinaigrettes
     emulsion, making an, 114–15
     Balsamic Vinaigrette, 96
     Caesar Dressing, 132
     Ginger Vinaigrette, 110
     Lemon Vinaigrette, 90
     Lemon Yogurt Dressing, 94
     Orange Vinaigrette, 106
     Pepperoncini Vinaigrette, 95
     Poppy Seed Dressing, 112
     Sesame Dressing, 100
     Sherry Vinaigrette, 98
     Sweet and Tangy Vinaigrette, 122
     White Balsamic Vinaigrette, 105
     Yogurt Green Goddess, 124

salami, in Italian Antipasto Rice Salad with
     Tuna and Egg, 95
salmon
     Japanese Breakfast with Spinach, Salmon,
          and Sweet Miso Dressing, 61
     Quinoa and Poached Salmon Salad with
          Confetti Vegetables, 90
     Salmon Poke Bowl with Brown Rice
          and Edamame, 130
     in Vietnamese Bowl with Sweet and
          Tangy Vinaigrette, 120
**Salmon Poke with Brown Rice and
     Edamame, 130**
**Sambal Tofu Quinoa Bowl with Sesame
     Spring Veggies, 119**
**Satay Bowl with Coconut Rice, Chicken
     or Tofu, 138**
Savory Yogurt, 203
     Indian Cauliflower and Chickpea Curry
          with Millet and, 202
Scallion Rice. See Ginger Scallion Rice
scissors, 25
seafood. See also salmon; shrimp; tuna
     about, 20–21
Sesame Dressing, 100
Sesame Duck and Wild Rice Salad, 100
**Sesame Spring Veggies, Sambal Tofu
     Quinoa Bowl with, 119**
**Shaved Brussels Sprouts with Spelt,
     Walnuts, and Pecorino, 98**
Sherry Vinaigrette, 98
shopping tips, 19–23
shrimp
     Baja BBQ Shrimp Bowl with Corn
          Rice, 199
     Red Rice Pad Thai with Tofu and
          Shrimp, 182
**Slow-Cooked Brown Rice and Quinoa
     Porridge, 68**
Slow-Roasted Tomatoes, 56
     Rice Bowl with Poached Egg, Feta,
          and, 55
     in Spiced Rice and Lentils with Seared
          Halloumi, 141
Smoky Tomato Salsa, 193
     in Ultimate Burrito Bowl, 192
snap peas
     in Sambal Tofu Quinoa Bowl with
          Sesame Spring Veggies, 119
     in Sticky Rice and Apple Slaw, 163
sorghum
     about, 43–44
     in Pastrami and Rye Berry Hash with
          Mustard Greens and Pickled Mustard
          Seeds, 73
     Sorghum Greek Salad, 105
Sorghum Greek Salad, 105

Sorghum Risotto Primavera with Bacon
and Burrata, 205
Sourmash Apple Crisp with Whole-Grain
Crisp Topping, 217
spatulas, 27
spelt
about, 44
Shaved Brussels Sprouts with Spelt,
Walnuts, and Pecorino, 98
Spiced Apple Breakfast Farro with Yogurt
Cream, 72
Spiced Rice and Lentils, 143
with Seared Halloumi, 141
Spicy Tuna Tartare with Brown Sushi Rice
and Avocado, 126
Spinach, Salmon, and Sweet Miso
Dressing, Japanese Breakfast with, 61
"steaming" milk or cream, 229
Sticky Rice and Apple Slaw, 163
Five-Spice Riblets with, 160
strainers, 31
Summer Corn Farrotto with Brown Butter
and Sweet Burst Tomatoes, 144
Sunday Night Detox Bowl with Roasted
Broccoli and Ponzu, 186
sunflower seeds
Grandmother Birdie's Oatmeal Cocktail
with Raisins and Salty Sunflower
Seeds, 50
in Rainbow Carrot Salad with Millet,
Feta, and Lemon Yogurt Dressing, 93
in Whole-Grain White Chocolate
Compost, 225
Sweet and Salty Granola with Toasted
Coconut and Pecans, 75
Sweet and Tangy Vinaigrette, 122
Vietnamese Bowl with, 120
Sweet Miso Dressing, 63
Japanese Breakfast with Spinach, Salmon,
and, 61
Sweet Potatoes, Coconut Curry Rice Bowl
with Green Vegetables and, 164

Tahini Sauce, 148
Burnt Vegetable Bowl with Black Rice
and Lentils and, 147
teff
about, 44
Flourless Chocolate Teff Cake, 218
in Four Grain "Nutella" Porridge with
Toasted Hazelnuts and Jam, 64
Mole Teff and Chicken with Avocado
and Crema, 174
tempering eggs, 229
Thai Peanut Sauce, 139
Toasted Millet Frozen Custard with Pan-
Seared Fruit, 230

tofu
Red Rice Pad Thai with Tofu and
Shrimp, 182
Sambal Tofu Quinoa Bowl with Sesame
Spring Veggies, 119
Tofu Satay Bowl with Coconut Rice,
138
in Vietnamese Bowl with Sweet and
Tangy Vinaigrette, 120
tomatoes. See also Slow-Roasted Tomatoes
Smoky Tomato Salsa, 193
in Sorghum Greek Salad, 105
Summer Corn Farrotto with Brown
Butter and Sweet Burst Tomatoes, 144
tongs, 27, 29
tools, 25–31
tossing a salad, 93
tuna
Italian Antipasto Rice Salad with Tuna
and Egg, 95
Spicy Tuna Tartare with Brown Sushi
Rice and Avocado, 126
turkey
Asian Breakfast Porridge with Turkey
Meatballs, 76
Chile En Nogada Bowl with Turkey
Picadillo and Walnut Crema, 178
turnips
in Graveyard Rice with Bone Marrow
and Parsley Salad, 151
in Moroccan Millet with Braised Root
Vegetables and Harissa, 157
Tzatziki, 185
Mezze Bowl with Pomegranate-Glazed
Lamb Meatballs, Hummus, and, 183

Ultimate Burrito Bowl, 192
Umbrian Farro and Bean Salad
with Celery Leaf Pesto, and Mozzarella,
103

vegetable peelers, 30
vegetables. See also specific vegetables
about, 19–20
Pickled Vegetables, 135
Vietnamese Bowl with Sweet and Tangy
Vinaigrette, 120
vinaigrettes. See salad dressings and
vinaigrettes
Vitamix blenders, 26

Walnut Crema, 180
Chile En Nogada Bowl with Turkey
Picadillo and, 178
walnuts
toasting, 69

Dark Chocolate Farro Goop with
Toasted Walnuts and Steamed Cream,
228
in Rosemary Buckwheat Crunch with
Fresh Ricotta, 70
Shaved Brussels Sprouts with Spelt,
Walnuts, and Pecorino, 98
Warm Chicken Caesar Bowl with Quinoa
and Kale, 131
warming oil, 73
wheat berries
about, 45
Deconstructed Italian Easter Pie with
Wheat Berries and Honey, 224
whisks, 29
White Balsamic Vinaigrette, 105
whole grains. See also specific grains
about, 32–45
author's experience with, 13–15
health benefits of, 32, 34
Whole-Grain Crisp Topping, 216
Mixed Berry Crisp with, 215
Whole-Grain White Chocolate Compost,
225
wild rice
about, 45
Coconut Black and Wild Rice Pudding
with Mangoes and Macadamia Nuts,
212
in Pastrami and Rye Berry Hash with
Mustard Greens and Pickled Mustard
Seeds, 73
Sesame Duck and Wild Rice Salad, 100
Winter Wild Rice Salad with Dates and
Parmesan, 106
Winter Wild Rice Salad with Dates and
Parmesan, 106

Yogurt Cream, 72
Spiced Apple Breakfast Farro with, 72
Yogurt Green Goddess, 124
Farmers' Market Bowl with Salty Pepitas
and, 123
Yogurt Lemon Dressing, 94
Rainbow Carrot Salad with Millet, Feta,
and, 93

zucchini
in Burnt Vegetable Bowl with Black Rice
and Lentils and Tahini Sauce, 147